THE GENEROSITY OF ACCEPTANCE

Volume I

THE GENEROSITY OF ACCEPTANCE

Volume I

Understanding Eating Difficulties in Children

Edited by

Gianna Williams, Paul Williams,
Jane Desmarais, & Kent Ravenscroft

Routledge
Taylor & Francis Group
LONDON AND NEW YORK

First published 2003 by Karnac Books Ltd

Published 2019 by Routledge
2 Park Square, Milton Park, Abingdon, Oxon OX14 4RN
52 Vanderbilt Avenue, New York, NY 10017

First issued in hardback 2019

Routledge is an imprint of the Taylor & Francis Group, an informa business

British Library Cataloguing in Publication Data

A C.I.P. for this book is available from the British Library

ISBN 13: 978-0-367-10735-2 (hbk)
ISBN 13: 978-1-85575-934-3 (pbk)

Edited, designed, and produced by Communication Crafts

CONTENTS

ACKNOWLEDGEMENTS

The editors would like to give special thanks to Lyndsay Macdonald for her invaluable work on the two volumes, and to Holly Barton, John Shaw, and Jessica Sully for their assistance with preparing the typescripts and proofs. We would also like to mention Andrea Chandler, at the Library of the Institute of Psychoanalysis, for her cheerful assistance with last-minute references.

EDITORS AND CONTRIBUTORS

Stephen Briggs is Senior Clinical Lecturer in Social Work and Vice Dean in the Adolescent Department of the Tavistock Clinic, London. He is the author of *Growth and Risk in Infancy* (Jessica Kingsley, 1997) and *Working with Adolescents: A Contemporary Psychodynamic Approach* (Palgrave, 2002). He has been a member of the Eating Disorders Workshop in the Adolescent Department.

Maria Antonietta Catena has a degree in Education and has taught for many years in one of Rome's most enlightened primary schools. She has attended, in Rome, the course in Psychoanalytic Observational Studies accredited by the Tavistock Clinic.

Jane Desmarais is Lecturer in English and Art History, working in the departments of English & Comparative Literature and History at Goldsmiths College, University of London. She is the author of *The Beardsley Industry* (Ashgate, 1998) and author and editor of other books, essays, and articles on the nineteenth century. She is currently writing *A Cultural History of Decadence* for Polity Press (2004), co-writing a book on cancer and psychoanalysis with Lawrence Goldie (Routledge, 2004), and has written (in the journal

Soundings, 18, 2001) on anorexia and passive resistance in Hermann Melville's 1853 tale, *Bartleby*. Her future projects include a book on skin, based on the work of Didier Anzieu's *Le Moi-Peau*.

Lynda Miller is a Consultant Child and Adolescent Psychotherapist at the Tavistock Clinic, where she is joint Head of the Learning Disability Service. She is also principal Child Psychotherapist at Enfield Child Guidance service and teaches on a clinical training in Bologna, Italy.

Selina Perocevic trained as a Clinical Psychologist at the University of Padua, Italy, and as Child and Adolescent Psychotherapist at the Tavistock Clinic. She works in an adolescent centre in North London (Brent Centre for Young People) and with children under 4 years old in South London (Sure Start). She teaches on the Tavistock Observational Studies and Infant Mental Health courses in Bristol.

Mariângela Mendes de Almeida Pinheiro is a Psychologist and Psychotherapist working in the mental health and child development fields in São Paulo, Brazil, from 1982. Between 1988 and 1993, she was a Clinical Associate at the Tavistock Clinic, where she wrote her MA thesis about early feeding difficulties, which was the basis for her chapter in this book.

Kent Ravenscroft was a Clinical Associate at the National Institute of Mental Health, where he trained in adolescent family therapy with Roger Shapiro, Helm Stierlin, and John Zinner. Trained in child and adult psychoanalysis at the Washington Psychoanalytic Institute, he is an Associate Clinical Professor at George Washington and Georgetown Medical Schools, where he formerly served as Training Director in Child and Adolescent Psychiatry, as well as Director of Family Therapy. He currently supervises and teaches on the Faculty of the International Institute of Object Relations Therapy and is in full-time private practice.

Maria Rhode is Consultant Child Psychotherapist and Professor of Child Psychotherapy at the Tavistock Clinic and University of East London. She is co-editor (with Margaret Rustin and Alex and

Hélène Dubinsky) of *Psychotic States in Children* (1997) and is presently co-editing, with Trudy Klauber, a book on Asperger's syndrome.

Gianna Williams has trained as a clinician for work with children and with adults. She has been on the teaching staff of the Tavistock Clinic since 1970 and subsequently became a Consultant Psychotherapist in the Adolescent Department of the Tavistock, where she founded the Eating Disorders Workshop in 1987. She is now co-organizing tutor of the Postgraduate Diploma MA in Working with People with Eating Disorders (Tavistock Clinic and University of East London). She has been a Visiting Professor at Pisa and Bologna Universities. She has founded numerous Tavistock Model courses in Italy, France, and Latin America. She has published widely in England and abroad, and her book, *Internal Landscapes and Foreign Bodies: Eating Disorders and Other Pathologies* (3rd edition, Karnac, 2002) has been translated into a number of languages, including Chinese.

Paul Williams is a member of the British Psychoanalytical Society and of the Royal Anthropological Institute. He is Joint Editor-in-Chief of the *International Journal of Psycho-Analysis* and Visiting Professor of Psychoanalysis at Anglia Polytechnic University, U.K. He has written widely on the subject of personality disorders and psychosis.

INTRODUCTION

> The receiver's capacity to be given to is a return gift to the original giver.
>
> E. Bott-Spillius, 1993

This book consists of a collection of chapters, selected by Gianna Williams with the assistance of Paul Williams, Jane Desmarais, and Kent Ravenscroft, written by current and past members of the Eating Disorders Workshop in the Adolescent Department of the Tavistock Clinic and by clinicians in Italy who have completed Tavistock-model courses in child and adolescent psychotherapy. All the patients were treated with a psychoanalytic approach, though there are variations in the frames of reference used by the authors. The chapters in Volume I are about work with children, while those in Volume II concentrate on adolescents. In spite of the different focus of each volume, there are many recurrent issues that connect the cases of children and adolescents. For example, many cases describe the anxieties and strategies of defence used against feelings of dependence and the risk of accepting from another. This is a core theme in both volumes and is the principal idea behind the paradoxical title, *The Generosity of Acceptance*. This title applies primarily to the struggle of some patients to accept from another, to become dependent on another, but it also refers to the need of clinicians to accept generously the sometimes violent projections of their patients. The gift of help often involves a risk of rejection, and the chapters in these two volumes vividly describe the courage and generosity it takes to persevere with patients suffering from serious eating disorders.

Psychoanalytic perspectives

Central to the psychoanalytic thinking behind the cases presented in these two volumes is a perspective principally defined by Melanie Klein's theory of object relations. This perspective may be divided, as far as these two books are concerned, into two main focuses: one relates to the reversal of the early dyadic relationship between mother and infant, the process defined by Wilfred Bion (1962a) as "container–contained"; the other relates to the failure to work through the oedipal situation. The two focuses are intimately related. In the first instance, Bion's notion of a container–contained relationship fails and is transformed, as Gianna Williams has noted, into a *receptacle–foreign-body* relationship. The infant or child is not only not contained, but is at the receiving end of parental projections. This is vividly illustrated in Chapter 6 of Volume I by the drawing entitled "An Exchange of Smoke between Houses". The smoke trails from the five houses, representing each member of the family, colliding in a vacuum. Everything, it is suggested here, is being emitted and projected, and nothing is being contained. For some, the introjection of projecting objects can become unbearable, and there is an imperative need to disgorge, emit, or block off these "missiles". Williams's accounts in *Internal Landscapes and Foreign Bodies* (1997) of the cases of Sally, a 17-year-old anorexic, and Daniel, an 18-year-old bulimic, illustrate a "no-entry" system of defences. So afraid of penetration of any kind, Sally revealed in her assessment a "vast array of 'no-entry' defences", which included finding the sound of the alarm clock and the telephone unbearable. Unable to cope with parents overflowing with projections, Daniel, a more "porous" patient than Sally, binged on white bread, which, when vomited, served as metaphorical blotting paper to mop up the mess of his internal world. The displacement of the chaos within to food that then can be brought up, discharged, projected, is striking in bulimics. In Volume II, writing from a different perspective, Ravenscroft describes "projective vomiting" in the case of the bulimic patient: "the bulimic uses expulsive elimination as an emergency manoeuvre—a psychosomatic defence" [Volume II, Chapter 3].

The second focus is concerned with the failure of triangulation—that is, a denial of the space within the dyadic couple and an accompanying wish and fear of fusion of subject and object. H. Boris (1984) and Diana Birksted-Breen (1989) have described the poverty of the "transitional" space in the anorexic's relationships and her desire for or fear of fusion with her mother, in particular. Marilyn Lawrence has developed this idea in "Loving Them to Death: The Anorexic and Her Objects" (2001). She describes the anorexic's terror of separateness and differentiation, and the concomitant need to control the objects of her internal and external worlds. Unable to symbolize and accept the inequalities and differences of human existence, the anorexic seeks to protect her oedipal illusions (in which mother and child constitute the central couple) and defend herself against unbearable pain and the anxieties of the depressive position.

The chapters in these two volumes explore the implications of both these obstacles to development for understanding the conditions of anorexia and bulimia, and several key themes emerge that shed light on some of the more central aspects of eating disorders. These may be identified as (1) failure in some aspects of early relationships; (2) fusion and projective identification; (3) attacks on the "paternal function"; and (4) the presence of an ego-destructive "superego" (Bion, 1962a).

The "fit" or "lack of fit" between mother and baby, for example, is a principal concern of Volume I. The work of G. Williams (1997) and Likierman (1997) is relevant here. They both emphasize the mutually destructive link between mother and child when needs remain unmet in infancy, and, drawing on Klein (1955), they connect a dread of dependence established in the early relationship with a desire later to obliterate otherness through fusion and projective identification. We see many instances of projective identification in the chapters of both volumes, but most notably in those in Volume II by Brough, Tirelli, Mondadori, Quagliata, and Petrelli. In this state of fusion between subject and object, what we might call the third element or the "paternal function"—the space between the dyadic relationship—is obliterated too. In both volumes, we encounter patients who exhibit an overwhelming desire to denigrate the actual father and, by extension, obliterate the intermediate space the father symbolically represents in the family relationship.

These characteristics make the therapeutic process very difficult and, as the clinicians in these two volumes demonstrate, the task of treating patients with eating disorders requires extraordinary patience and courage. This task is made more difficult by the presence of a destructive superego on the side of death that speaks to the patient and through the patient and engenders persecutory feelings that are potentially fatal. This is the voice described by Magagna in her chapter, "I Don't Want to Die, But I Have To". In the following sections, further consideration will be given to the ways in which individual chapters address these key themes.

Early relationships

Several chapters suggest or imply that the rejection of a feeling of dependence might be related to a failure in some aspects of early relationships. This failure is essentially the lack of fit between mother and child, meaning the absence of an ability to give and receive reciprocally. This lack of fit is given symbolization by Petrelli's patient [II, 8], who describes a "black button"—a sign of mourning—very reminiscent of the work of Frances Tustin (1972), and Petrelli suggests that this could be the "sign of the loss of the breast, an empty hole, something related to the lack of an early fit". This view is endorsed by Tirelli [II, 2] who also makes the case that the lack of the "function of receiving" (cf. Likierman, 1997), may be due to difficulties in weaning and achieving the depressive position. An emotional "misfit" due to an extreme lack of boundaries and separateness is described in the first chapter of Volume I by Miller, in her account of a two-year infant observation of Jenny and her daughter, Anna. Here the breast could not be mourned because it became for Anna "a devalued and at times contemptible object". In Perocevic's chapter [I, 3], we learn that Miral, 6 years old, had refused food in infancy and later would only eat mashed food in front of the television, "one item at a time". Briggs [I, 4], too, suggests that his 9-year-old patient, George, might have experienced a "catastrophic weaning". George restricted the acceptable items of food to a minimum, and, like Miral, never ate more than one item at a time. In her chapter on "Aspects of the Body Image and Sense of Identity in a Boy with Autism", Rhode [I, 5] describes the re-enactment of a catastrophic birth experience when her patient, Anthony, falls off the desk and struggles to reach the safety of a chair. We shall return to this theme later when we consider the idea of triangular relationships.

In Volume I, Pinheiro [I, 2] describes two cases, one where the child did not accept food at all, and another where the child refused solids. In both these cases, there seems to be not only a lack of an early fit, but a double failure of containment—that is, a reversal of the container–contained relationship, resulting in a receptacle–foreign-body relationship. This is also the case of Perocevic [I, 3], whose patient was taken at the age of 10 days to hospital with a gastric problem and whose mother, unable to bear the anxiety, rushed out of the ambulance in a panic. This child clearly developed a no-entry system of defences (Williams, 1997) when used as a receptacle of parental projections. Pinheiro [I, 2] suggests that the infants' "capacity to signal their hunger might have been diminished in a context of parental unavailability to explore and try to understand the meaning of their crying".

In Volume II, which concentrates on adolescents and late-adolescents, there are many examples of failure in some aspects of early relationships. For instance, Mondadori's patient [II, 4], Lydia, had problems with food in primary school. We know nothing about the early relationships in the case of Yufang, the extremely regressed patient of Magagna [II, 5], but it is as if we follow an infant observation in the detailed narrative of this case. The tiny amounts of Chinese food that are eventually acceptable to this patient affected by pervasive refusal syndrome are virtually baby food. In these two volumes, it is possible to formulate a hypothesis about early failures of containment and other problems going back to the nursing couple, even when factual information about the history is not available. The generosity of acceptance, crucial to a healthy feeding relationship, may not be possible because of a severe dread of dependence, and one of the ways of avoiding receiving from another is to obliterate otherness by projective identification and fusion.

Fusion and projective identification

Petrelli [II, 8] describes the relationship that her patient, Ivana, wished to have with both her mother and also with Petrelli herself in the transference as "growing old together trapped in a kind of paralyzed equilibrium". The fusion is idealised but deadly. Lack of separateness is graphically shown by Perocevic's chapter [I, 3], in which the family of four are described as sleeping in the same room as the grandparents. The family found great obstacles in leaving the grandparents' house although separate premises were available. In the patient himself, Miral, lack of separateness takes the form of massive projective identification. He is constantly inside the object, rather than with it. This mode has a clearly defensive function for him, as *being with* implies the unbearable experience of *being without* when the object is absent. Miral's intolerance of separation and separateness is also evident in the transference to his therapist.

Projective identification is a significant feature of the chapter by Quagliata [II, 6], where the patient constantly migrates from one identity to another to the extent of becoming depersonalized. Her functioning, like Mondadori's Lydia, is strikingly reminiscent of that described in Klein's paper, "On Identification" (Klein, 1955). In this paper, quoted by Mondadori, Klein refers to a novel where the main character is allowed to take over the identity of anyone he envies, as long as he keeps his own name in his pocket as a sort of return ticket into his own identity. Quagliata's patient, Deborah, often appears to lose her sense of identity in her projective identification and clearly does not keep her name in her pocket. The definition, "intrusive identification" (Meltzer, 1986), would apply to Deborah. She even intrudes in her analyst's space and time by leaving countless telephone messages on her answering machine between sessions. This case supports Lawrence's hypothesis (Lawrence, 2001) that anxieties about being intruded upon in patients with eating disorders may be due to a projection of their own intrusiveness.

Loss of identity is the high price many patients pay in order to avoid the experience of separateness and dependence, acknowledgement of which would involve a costly feeling of gratitude. An arresting example of lack of identity is given in Mondadori's chapter [I, 4], where we see the patient literally step into the "manager's shoes" at a time when she starts working in a shoe shop. When her state of projective identification lessens, Lydia very graphically gets rid of the many characters she has impersonated by donating to Oxfam thirty-six pairs of shoes.

Confusion of identity between patient and mother—"I am you and you are me"—is also described in the chapter by Rhode [I, 5], in which she refers to an anorexic patient's phantasy of starving in order to harm her mother. Brough [II, 1] describes her patient, Rebecca, as exhausting herself in cross-country running and as using her body to attack her mother, with whom she is identified. In a large number of cases of anorexia, the patient is in projective identification with the mother's body and attacks it by means of his or her starvation.

Freud provides a striking example of this type of phantasized attack on another in his famous case study of the "Rat Man":

> One day while he [the patient] was away on his summer holiday the idea suddenly occurred to him that he was too fat [German *dick*] and he must *make himself slimmer.* So he began getting up from the table before the pudding came round and tearing along the road without a hat in the blazing heat of the August sun. Then he would dash up a mountain at the double, till, dripping with perspiration, he was forced to come to a stop. ... Our patient could think of no explanation of this senseless, obsessional behaviour until it suddenly occurred to him that at that time his lady had also been stopping at the same resort; but she had been in the company of an English

> cousin, who was very attentive to her and of whom the patient had been very jealous. This cousin's name was Richard, and, according to the usual practice in England, he was known as *Dick.* Our patient then had wanted to kill this Dick. [1909, pp. 188–189]

It seems that Freud's patient slips into the identity of his rival Dick and he attacks the "fat one" [*dick*] by exhausting himself. This is an interesting anticipation of the use of Klein's concept of projective identification.

In the case of Aurora, described by Tirelli [II, 2], we see the patient eventually becoming more separate and we follow the difficult route that leads to this achievement. In witnessing the magnitude of the struggle to achieve separateness and accept a relationship of healthy dependence, we as clinicians can better appreciate the magnitude of the defences mobilized against psychic pain and envy. They offer protection from depressive feelings, such as gratitude (Klein, 1952), which are engendered in relationships where there is "generosity of acceptance". We are also helped to understand the extent of the control exercised by many eating disorders patients. This is described in many of the chapters, but particularly in Dubinsky's [I, 7]. Her patient, Julie, achieves spasmodic control over her food and over her objects, but also, as Dubinsky points out, primarily over her needs and her needy self. In this case, the control is chiefly exercised in order not to experience the threat of needing another or depending on another.

Attacks on the paternal function and the couple

The states of mind of fusion and projective identification obliterate the differentiation between the subject and the object. Siamese twins, it has been observed, may be aware of their sibling as "another" because there is some physical space that separates them. The equivalent of this space, the emotional space, between "you and me", is obliterated in the state of mind of fusion. An important distinction, however, needs to be made here. In a relationship of two people, a dyadic relationship, there is always a third element—that is, the space between them—and in a state of mind of fusion that space is lacking. A dyadic relationship is therefore in effect always triadic, the third element being constituted of the space between the subject and object. The term "dyadic" might imply twoness in its etymology, but in its application the term actually refers to a triadic relationship (Williams & Judd, 2002).

This third element may be referred to as the "paternal function", whether this function is performed by the mother herself or the actual father or is the provision of a boundary between mother and child. It is important to underline that this is a *function* and not necessarily a *person*. In many of the cases where fusion, lack of separateness, and projective identification are present, there is a strong attack on the paternal function. This can take a violent form, as in the case of Mondadori's Lydia [I, 4], who cut out the father from all the family photographs, and who brought this attack on the paternal function into the transference relationship. Mondadori notes: "Since I was in control of her time, I ceased to be a supportive and available mother for her. I became instead a cold and rejecting father figure whom she wanted to cut out of her life." Something similar is described by Brough [II, 1] when she observed that her patient, Rebecca, "looked at her or watched her when she was thinking" because "she didn't seem to know what was happening". This description can be linked to the one given by Britton in his 1989 paper "The Missing Link", in which the patient perceives the analyst's thinking as an internal dialogue, an intercourse within the analyst's mind. Wishing to stop it, or at least interfere with it, Britton's patient exclaims, "Stop that fucking thinking!"

The clinicians in these two volumes give many examples of the attack on the paternal function. It is present in the here-and-now of the transference relationship, but it is also present in references to the actual father whom the patient so often wishes to obliterate. In Mondadori's case [II, 3], the onset of anorexia may have been intimately connected with the separation of the patient's parents, a "mission accomplished" in Lydia's phantasy which could have evoked in her persecutory guilt.

In some cases, not only the presence, but the very existence of the father seems to be obliterated. Perocevic's patient [I, 3], Miral, uses skin colour as proof that his father does not exist. Miral, whose skin was white like that of his mother, used this perception to confirm that he was totally at one with his mother. This helped him to deny the existence of his father as a parent, as he had a different skin colour. At times the father is a rather shadowy figure. In Petrelli's chapter [II, 8], the father is described as a weak man, withdrawn into himself, suffering from epilepsy, and perceived by the patient as more of a child rival than a paternal presence. The paternal function also seems conspicuous by its absence in the case described by Ravenscroft [II, 3]. Mother is unable to set any boundaries to the patient, Paula, although she feels that "she did not have enough milk to satisfy a demanding, all-consuming, bottomless pit" which was "running her ragged". Anxious about being restricting and ungiving, like her own mother, and fearing Paula's anger and rejection, she never limits or denies Paula food or social licence.

At times we have no objective evidence of the lack of the paternal function, but we see a marked denigration of the father and the parental couple in the patients' material. This is evident in Brough's Rebecca [II, 1], who turned the parental intercourse into something that could only be damaging to mother—indeed, the cause of her depression. Rebecca develops an obsession with her father's snoring at night. This could be a denigration of "primal-scene" noises. It is not unusual in eating disorders for the patient to describe the father as making "animal" or "disgusting" noises when eating.

It is difficult to imagine a more inappropriate couple, less likely to unite and perform a creative intercourse, than the "frog and the goldfish" of Briggs's patient, George [I, 4]. It is clear that this patient's feeding difficulties are an attempt to keep the parents separate, as separate as the items of food on his plate. Like Miral [I, 3 (Perocevic)], George eats one item at a time, and never two together; so, for instance, never bread with parmesan or pasta with parmesan. His parents had to be kept separate since, when mother and father came together, they were experienced by him as terrifying, persecutory figures threatening his survival (cf. Britton, 1998).

Rhode's Anthony [I, 5] also seems to experience the parents as uniting against him to form a cruel and impervious object. When he sits between them, he smiles in a way that Rhode perceives as cruel, not joining the parents but separating them. This child has very complex phantasies connected with his difficulties with food. "Eating and growing ... is confused with separating a parental couple. By implication, the child ... makes himself vulnerable to be devoured by the parents when they come together." The child makes a violent oral attack on the parents that turns them into a formidable devouring object.

The ego-destructive superego

There seems to be, in the internal landscape of some of the patients described, a fierce presence that caricatures a paternal function and masquerades as a moral imperative. This has been termed, following Bion (1962a), the ego-destructive superego, and there are many instances of its presence in the "internal landscapes" of some of these patients. We meet a less extreme version of this superego in Marco's "policeman" [I, 6 (Catena)], and in Ivana's second mouth [II, 8 (Petrelli)], and the placation of a harsh superego is described in Dubinsky's chapter [II, 7]: "a bargain had been struck—if she starved herself it would stop the incessant accusations and demands from within". We meet a very ominous superego in Magagna's patient, Yufang [I, 5], as it is the voice of the destructive superego that speaks through her when she says: "I don't want to die, but I have to." This superego engenders persecutory feelings of guilt in the patient that make reparation impossible. A benign parental or paternal function (i.e. a benign superego) helps to sustain the hope that reparation is possible.

We might conclude where we began, with the idea that underpins these two volumes on the generosity of acceptance. In every case described, reparation is only possible when there is a flow of giving and receiving between patient and clinician. Profound anxieties about the preservation of life are often split off and projected by patients into almost intolerable attacks on the analyst, who may feel bombarded and under siege. The relationship between "giver" and "receiver" in clinical work is described with a richness of modulation in E. Bott-Spillius's article, "Varieties of Envious Experience" (1993).

The *return gift*, as demonstrated by the careful work observed in these two volumes, is to receive—and to receive generously. The degree of patience, courage, and open-heartedness that this requires from clinicians is perhaps a defining characteristic of the task of treating patients with eating disorders.

Gianna Williams
Paul Williams
Jane Desmarais
Kent Ravenscroft

THE GENEROSITY OF ACCEPTANCE

Volume I

CHAPTER ONE

Idealization and contempt: dual aspects of the process of devaluation of the breast in a feeding relationship

Lynda Miller

It is ironic and perhaps also rather sad that a retrospective reading-through of my mother and infant observations, which comprised an essential part of my pre-clinical training, led me to formulate the title of this chapter. The irony and sadness lie, I think, in the contrast, described in this chapter, between the mother's highly idealized conscious ideas about breast-feeding, and the less conscious and unconscious processes by which the breast seemed to become a devalued and at times contemptible object for her baby.

I observed this mother, Jenny, with her baby, Anna, on a weekly basis over a period of two years, and subsequently on infrequent occasions. At the time of Anna's birth, Jenny and her boyfriend Michael, both of whom are Australian, were living in a "commune" in a large semi-derelict house with a group of friends. Inside, the room shared by the couple was brightly painted and well cared for, and the parents-to-be were adamant that their first child would be born in their home with as little medical intervention as possible.

At my first meeting with Jenny and Michael, they emphasized to me their particular views on child-rearing, and they both seemed to adhere quite rigidly to an "alternative" ideology by which certain ideas and practices were deemed good as opposed to others that were seen as extremely bad. To give some of the most relevant examples: Jenny felt that a hospital birth would inevitably produce a traumatized and damaged baby, and she warned me that observations might be impeded by the fact that she intended to carry the baby next to her body all the time. She also made frequent references to the diet that she followed, consisting of a very limited range of health foods that she felt were "pure" as opposed to the "contaminated" food—in particular, any animal product—eaten by most people in our culture.

In accord with the parents' wishes, Anna was born at home among a circle of close friends. Jenny gave birth in a supported squatting position, and after seven hours of labour Anna was delivered into a bath of warm water and, in Jenny's words, "lay there smiling, looking all around". Jenny reported triumphantly that no drugs at all had been needed, and that the fight she had anticipated having with her doctor if he tried to make her take a drug to expel the placenta had not even been necessary, as it had come away naturally.

A most significant aspect of this anti-orthodox ideology was the belief apparently held by Jenny that the breast would provide for all Anna's needs and would serve to maintain a blissful state of fusion between mother and baby, almost as if the separative act of birth could be nullified. Accordingly, the breast was always available to Anna throughout day and night, and she was not yet fully weaned at 3½ years of age. The popular term "demand feeding" is not truly applicable here, as Jenny would offer Anna the breast whenever she showed any sign of distress, even when a feed did not seem at all to be what the baby had in mind.

I have selected observations that I hope will illustrate the qualities that for me characterize the feeding relationship of this nursing couple, with particular reference to the fate of the mother's aspiration to achieve and sustain an idealized symbiotic fusion with her baby. I shall begin with some excerpts from the very earliest observations following the birth.

Anna was just 13 days old and Jenny had been feeding her almost every hour, just offering one breast at each feed time in order, in Jenny's words, "not to break the natural flow and rhythm of the sucking".

> The baby looked very relaxed held in Jenny's arms . . . her face became increasingly red and bloated, eyes more closed yet never fully as the feed progressed. She seemed to stare upwards or towards the breast, not at Jenny's face. Jenny did not speak at all. . . . She focused intently on the baby all the time. At one point the baby made an "Aaa" soft sighing sound, and Jenny echoed this.

Later in the same observation, following her feed at one breast, Anna was lying across Jenny's lap gazing up at her:

> The baby made little sounds, and Jenny gently moved her around, sometimes echoing her, saying "Aaa" very softly. The baby gave a sudden loud cry followed by panting, and Jenny said "Oh, you want some more?" lifting her sweater and offering the other breast which the baby took eagerly, sucking intently, very still and quiet. After a few minutes the baby no longer appeared to be sucking, yet lay still with the nipple in her mouth.

Although here Jenny had a fixed preconception in her mind about offering only one breast, she was sufficiently receptive and flexible to be able to learn from her baby's communications and to respond by offering both breasts consecutively from then on. In these first few weeks of Anna's life, despite exhaustion, Jenny seemed to be totally absorbed in her baby and to feel sustained by an experience of "at oneness", unfractured by any sense of separateness.

By the time Anna was 23 days old there were already indications, observed in the following extract, that the harmonious quality of this feeding relationship was under threat:

> Anna began to cry a little, making small "Aaa" sounds, some quite deep and full. Jenny described to me how her mother had visited last week, which had "got under her skin" and made her irritable, and she was sure the baby had picked up her mood.

> Anna cried more loudly, vigorously kicking her legs and clenching her fists. Jenny said to her, "I've been a grumpy mummy haven't I? What is it you want? Is it a feed?" She unbuttoned her dress, and Anna immediately turned her head to the nipple and sucked vigorously, panting at first and making little sounds with each suck. Anna suddenly let go of the nipple and turned her head away from the breast, and Jenny lifted her and turned her around, offering the other breast. At first Anna sharply turned her head away, then took the nipple when Jenny held it between two of her fingers. Anna continued to suck vigorously, sometimes making a loud kissing sound with her lips. Her cheeks became increasingly red and bloated and her eyes glazed and shining. After a few more minutes sucking, Anna began to turn her head rapidly from side to side, a small but quick repeated movement. I could not see but I think her mouth was alternately making and losing contact with the nipple. Jenny said "Is this a game, eh?" but whenever she tried to move Anna away from the breast, Anna gave a loud cry. She became more distressed, kicking her legs hard, beating her arms up and down, intermittently turning her head to and fro. Jenny said "Have you had enough?" but Anna cried louder still. She did not seem to want the breast, yet she could not relinquish it, repeatedly turning towards it, then away. Jenny said to me, "This is the worst bit, when I just don't know what she wants. She seems to live in her own world and screams when she has finished feeding."

It seemed that misunderstandings were beginning to arise between mother and baby. In a number of my observations of the first few months, a pattern emerged in which Anna would turn repeatedly towards and away from the breast when it was offered and she did not necessarily want to suckle. Anna's experience of the breast clearly did not always match Jenny's idealization, and she seemed through her ambivalence to be challenging her mother's belief that the breast could ameliorate any painful feelings.

In her paper "Envy and Gratitude", Melanie Klein (1957) stressed the importance of differentiating between a good object and an idealized object. Although this distinction cannot be absolute, she states: "A very deep split between the two aspects of the object indicates that it is not the good and the bad object that are being kept apart but an idealized and an extremely bad one. So deep and sharp a division reveals that destructive impulses, envy and persecutory anxiety are very strong and that idealization serves mainly as a defence against these emotions" (p. 192). When the split is not excessive, the processes of ego integration and object synthesis so necessary for healthy development can come into operation, allowing identification with a good object to become established.

From the flavour of the observation described above, strong persecutory elements seemed to be present, evidenced especially in Anna's screaming following a feed. In Klein's view (1957): "Excessive idealisation denotes that persecution is the main driving force . . . idealisation is a corollary of persecutory anxiety—a defence against it—and the ideal breast is the counterpart of the devouring breast" (p. 193).

Furthermore, the distressed, repetitive manner in which Anna turned to and from the breast suggested a confused state of mind, not typical of the developmental sort of splitting that leads to a capacity to discriminate between goodness and badness. This baby's confusion could perhaps be understood in terms of a projective identification with her mother's state of mind. Jenny's tendency towards excessive splitting can clearly be seen in her attitudes towards many aspects of her life—food in particular, as described earlier. Mrs Klein (1957) speaks of an incapacity to possess a good object, which is dealt with by means of idealization, and which "is also bound up with the confusion between good and bad that arises in the relation to the primal object" (p. 193). She adds in a footnote that the mother–baby relation is particularly idealized by ". . . those people who were not able to experience sufficient happiness in this relation" (p. 193). I think this may have been the case for this mother, and I will elaborate upon this later. With regard to the baby, it seemed that she was in collusion with her mother's idealization of the breast, thereby also being prone to experiencing the intensely persecutory aspect of her object, especially, as I gathered from Jenny, during the night.

Since her birth Anna had always slept in the same bed as her parents. She awoke frequently throughout the night, and Jenny would always give her the breast to pacify her. Usually she would quieten and fall asleep again, but on some occasions Jenny told me that Anna would refuse the breast and scream relentlessly.

When Anna was 6 weeks old, Jenny related an incident that had taken place the previous night and which highlighted for me the parents' belief in a sensual, physical mode of containment. Jenny described how on one particularly bad night when Anna had been screaming for half an hour, she and Michael managed eventually to soothe her by taking off all their clothes and giving Anna "a really close cuddle", sandwiching her between their naked bodies.

When Anna was a few months old a small room became vacant in the house, and this was allocated to the new family. Mother and baby continued to share a bed in the larger room while father moved into the new room to sleep. The physical closeness between Jenny and Anna was sustained throughout most of the day, because Jenny carried Anna in a front sling as a small baby and, when she grew heavier, in a back-pack. Thus eye-to-eye contact between mother and baby was minimal.

During the early months of her life, the expression I saw most often on Anna's face was a rather dreamy, hazy one; she would gaze into space and did not often seek or respond to direct eye contact. This is from an observation when Anna was 1½ months old:

> I sat Anna on my lap and she turned her head towards me and looked up but not directly at me. She held onto my fingers loosely, moving her fingertips rhythmically. Her eyes moved a little from side to side, focused in my direction but seeming to avoid my eyes and face.

Where the emphasis is placed so heavily upon physical holding, as with this mother and baby, rather than upon an experience of being held in mind, of being looked at and talked to by a mother who wants to get to know her baby, it is possible that development might be hindered in some respects. A superficial "adhesive" kind of identification precludes the dimension of depth prerequisite for discovery and the growth of knowledge. In "adhesive identification", the infant feels itself to be held together only when it is attached to its object, and I think that this term is applicable to some extent to this mother and baby.

Esther Bick, in her well-known paper on infant observation (1964),[1] gives examples of two different ways in which mothers and babies relate to each other: first, a mode that is predominantly visual and vocal; second, one in which tactile and kinaesthetic communication is preferred. Although either mode can provide a satisfactory basis for containment and growth, clearly both are essential in varying degrees for a baby's potential to unfold, and one should not totally preclude the other.

For Jenny and Anna, as the latter's experience of containment relied so strongly upon the uninterrupted sensation of mouth-to-nipple and skin-to-skin contact, it became almost impossible for Jenny to put her down without Anna becoming very distressed. In this observation (Anna, 1½ months), following a feed, Jenny was carrying Anna in her arms, walking around the room and patting her back:

> Anna's head flopped right over to one side on Jenny's shoulder, and her eyelids kept drooping and closing. She then seemed to be trying to keep them open. This happened a few times then she fell asleep. Jenny said "amazing—I'll give her five minutes" and very gently lowered her down, head first into a basket on the floor. While being lowered Anna suddenly moved her arms out and spread her fingers as if experiencing a sensation of falling.

Perhaps Anna lost her sense of being held together in one piece when the contact of her body with her mother's body was broken.

[1] Esther Bick introduced infant observation into the training of child psychotherapists at the Tavistock Clinic. As a training method, it consists of regular one-hour weekly observations made on an infant and his or her caretakers in their home setting, from birth, usually for two years. The observer is encouraged to maintain a receptive, non-intrusive, non-judgmental, attentive presence, while closely observing the early relationship development between infant, mother, and other members of the family. This method requires the observer to be attentive to his or her own states of mind while in contact with such primitive emotional states in the infant and his or her family, and to allow this experience to make its own impact (Briggs, 1993; Miller, Rustin, Rustin, & Shuttleworth, 1989).

The next week, when Anna had again just fallen asleep in Jenny's arms and was being lowered into her basket,

> Anna's eyes remained closed but her breathing became louder and she rapidly opened and closed her fists. As her head touched the bottom of the basket her eyes flickered open. Jenny placed her hand on Anna's head and bent right over her. Anna looked up at Jenny and made little whimpering sounds. After a few minutes, Jenny tried to withdraw her hand and began to speak to me, but immediately Anna's eyes opened wide. She screwed up her face and cried loudly.

Anna would not be pacified, and when Jenny offered the breast, guiding Anna's mouth to the nipple, she refused it with a cry of protest:

> Anna's left hand was near to the nipple, and she appeared to be grabbing and pinching the breast as she pushed it away and arched back.

Edna O'Shaughnessy (1964) utilizes Bion's ideas in describing a feature of an infant's relationship to the breast in its presence and in its absence. She suggests that "When the infant feels hungry and in need of the breast, he is aware of a need not satisfied. This frustration, the pain of his hunger, is what is present to him, and this, initially, is felt as a bad breast present" (p. 35).

Perhaps for Anna, the proximity of her mother's body, with a focus on the breast, had become almost indispensable because she had very rarely been allowed to experience any frustration and thus to begin to deal with an absent object. On the occasions when Jenny does try to put Anna down to sleep by herself, it could be that a phantasy of a bad breast is projected into the actual breast when it reappears, because no time is allowed for Anna to process this experience at a mental level. Anna is in fact being deprived of the experience of an absent object because Jenny so readily offers the breast at the first sign of frustration. In O'Shaughnessy's view, this would not be conducive to the development of thinking.

In the months that followed there did seem to be a lessening of the undifferentiated, collusive elements in the relationship, at least in part initiated by Anna as in the following excerpt (Anna, 2 months, 1 week):

> Anna made little sounds which gradually became closer to cries, arching her head back and waving her outside arm. Jenny lifted her sweater saying "You know what's coming don't you?" and offered the breast. Anna did not turn her head towards the nipple, so Jenny gently guided her there. Anna took the nipple in her mouth but did not seem to suck, her hands fingering Jenny's sweater.

Jenny interpreted to Anna that she just wanted the experience, not any milk, adding softly "You don't care at all do you? You don't care." And a few minutes later:

> Jenny pulled up her sweater and offered the breast saying "here it is" then "you don't prefer your fingers do you?" when Anna seemed to be trying to cram her fist into her mouth and did not take the breast.

At 7½ months, Anna was able to pull herself to a standing position and took a triumphant delight in this independent achievement. Jenny congratulated her with great pleasure, and there seemed to be a lessening in the adhesive quality of their contact and more signs of Anna achieving a degree of ego integration.

At the same time, on "bad" days I saw quite a different side of Anna. One observation took place entirely on Jenny's bed on a day when she seemed especially tired and dejected:

> Anna continued to play with the brush, vocalizing quietly and frequently looking up at me. Jenny curled up on her side behind Anna and appeared to fall asleep instantly. Without turning around, Anna suddenly dropped the brush and reached out behind herself with her arm extended until she touched Jenny, toppling over as she did so . . . she grabbed at Jenny's nose and pulled it, then at her lips, trying to grip them firmly. Later, Anna grabbed at her lips and nose again, and Jenny sighed and said "Is it time for titty again?" Anna grabbed at Jenny's blouse, and as soon as Jenny had undone the buttons she grasped the

> nipple and pulled it into her mouth, sucking hard and noisily. With her outside arm she reached for the other breast, and when Jenny pulled open her blouse fully, Anna grasped the other nipple, fingering and pulling at it while sucking the first breast.

On days like this Anna seemed to lose any sense of boundary between herself and her mother in a manner suggestive of projective identification, whereby in phantasy split-off parts of the self, or even the whole self, are projected into the mother or her breast. Moreover there was a notable correlation between Jenny's state of exhaustion and Anna's demands upon her mother, with little evidence of Anna developing a capacity to spare her mother when she was very tired. Anna apparently found it unbearable to have a depleted mother; this may have arisen out of a phantasy of having taken possession of the breast and of having sucked her mother dry, thereby causing her depletion.

O'Shaughnessy (1964) suggests that "an inability to separate from the object may be due to a fear of being alone with an internally damaged object without the reassurance of its external presence" (p. 40). If this were the case here, Anna would be driven to return again and again to the breast out of a need for self-reassurance and would therefore be incapable of developing the capacity for concern which would enable her mother to rest and recover.

Moreover, it was my impression that this situation was exacerbated by Michael's apparent failure to provide a firm paternal function of protecting Jenny and contributing to the bringing about of a good separation. The lack of father's active presence allowed the baby to intrude relentlessly into her mother. One could speculate that for Anna there would be a difficulty in internalizing a combined object, the absence of which would fuel persecutory anxiety in relation to the breast.

When Anna was 9½ months old, Jenny often complained of her being clinging and possessive. In the following observation, Anna had been holding onto her mother's legs and Jenny was clearly irritated by this. Wearily, she lifted Anna onto her lap and offered the breast:

> Anna sucked for a few seconds, then turned right away to stare at me, still smiling. She turned back to the breast and held onto the nipple with a pinching movement of her thumb and forefinger, but did not attempt to suck. She made little sounds and seemed restless. Jenny lifted her jumper up and down over the breast, saying "here it is", then "all gone". Anna watched her, smiling and interested, but did not make an active response.

There may have been an element of protest in Anna's unwillingness to accept the breast as a remedy for all discontents. For Jenny, Anna's lack of enthusiasm might be felt to be a rejection, inspiring an unconscious wish to turn the breast into a tantalizing and provocative object. Continuing from the above observation:

> Jenny put Anna down on the floor again. Anna turned towards Jenny and grabbed her legs again, and Jenny picked up the doll, saying "maybe Lucy wants some titty?" putting the doll to her breast and making sucking noises. Anna smiled uncertainly then turned away.

Anna had always been accustomed to unlimited access to the breast, and even at times when it was inconvenient for Jenny to feed her (in the excerpt below she wanted to wash her hair) she invariably gave in to Anna's demands, with an air of resignation:

> She whined and clung to Jenny's legs, and Jenny said with a sigh, "Oh, it's like that is it?" Anna grabbed at Jenny's sweater, reached down the front of it to her T-shirt, and pulled it down, searching for the breast. Having found it, after a few seconds she turned away and lost interest, picking up a cup which she thrust at Jenny's mouth then rubbed against her own lips. Jenny held the nipple between her thumb and forefinger, saying to Anna "Hey, don't you want this any more?" but Anna did not respond and continued playing with the cup, vocalizing loudly.

As O'Shaughnessy (1964) points out, "A child always, in part, wants even to be weaned", and for this nursing couple, I think the question arises as to whether it is the mother or the infant who cannot bear to face the painful feelings of loss that inevitably accompany weaning. Where boundaries are so blurred, it is difficult to imagine that either Jenny or Anna would be able to take a decisive step in the direction of separation.

In her account of the Kleinian theory of depression, Dina Rosenbluth (1965) states that "The loss of the close intimate contact with the feeding, holding, comforting mother, results in the narcissistic illusion of 'oneness' or 'fusion' with her being shattered" (p. 21). She is speaking here from the baby's point of view, but where the mother has not herself been able to work through adequately the conflicts of the depressive position, she may be unable to face them when they are reactivated acutely in her relationship with her own baby.

Rosenbluth (1965) describes the state of fusion as a narcissistic illusion. Perhaps the phantasy of being "at one" with her baby that Jenny strives to perpetuate can best be understood as an illusion, in that it conceals a hidden dynamic relationship in the form of mutual projective identification. Klein (1957) posits a significant link between idealization as a defence against persecution and excessive projective identification, a process by which split-off parts of the self are projected into the object, leading to "a strong confusion between the self and the object, which also comes to stand for the self" (p. 192).

By 11 months of age, Anna was beginning to achieve a measure of independence in some areas of her development, walking around by herself with much glee and readily engaging with other children and adults. However, while Anna was taking an active and lively interest in the world around her, having to share her mother and relinquish her position as sole owner of the breast posed conflicts she preferred to avoid. In this observation a little boy, Daniel, and his mother were visiting:

> Anna seemed intent on getting whatever Daniel had at the time. She got to her feet and pulled at Daniel's sheet of paper. He squealed in protest, and Anna began to cry loudly, turning to Jenny who was talking to Daniel's mother and appeared disinclined to feed Anna at that moment. Jenny carried on talking

> but Anna continued tugging at her sweater and crying. After a few minutes, Jenny lifted her sweater and Anna sucked hard at the breast, mostly with eyes closed, totally engrossed.

One week later, Jenny opened the front door holding Anna in her arms, fast asleep with the nipple in her mouth. She carried her carefully upstairs and lay down on the bed, falling asleep herself almost instantly. I sat beside the bed and watched Anna, who remained deeply asleep throughout the observation, still keeping the nipple in her mouth. At one point she stirred in her sleep and reached out an arm as if searching for the other breast. She made sucking movements with her lips for a few seconds, but she did not awaken or let go of the nipple.

Here Anna seemed to be using the breast as a "dummy", as an indispensable source of comfort. She was still sleeping with her mother at night, and, although the parents were busy decorating a separate bedroom for her, it was difficult to imagine how she would be able to make the transition to sleeping by herself. The sleeping arrangements of this family underline the lack of a boundary around the parental couple.

Throughout Anna's second year of life she continued to turn often to the breast during day and night, but on many occasions during my observations it seemed that the experience of breastfeeding aroused uncomfortable and at times distressing feelings in both mother and baby.

In this observation Anna (at 13½ months) had just climbed onto a chair, then slipped to the floor with a crash:

> Jenny carried Anna, still screaming, straight over to a chair and lifted her sweater, saying "Have some titty, that will make it better". Jenny held the nipple and guided Anna's mouth to it. For a second she turned her head away, looking at me with a red angry face, then she took the nipple in her mouth and sucked hard. With her free arm she was trying to push Jenny's sweater further up, as if somehow to get more of the breast. And with her feet she pushed and kicked at Jenny's arm and shoulder angrily. When she let go of the nipple later (after a few minutes) she was still crying, but then became quiet. Jenny

> turned her around to the other breast, but Anna would not take it, and her crying becoming louder. Turning her again, Jenny gave her the first breast and Anna sucked some more, still pushing Jenny's arm away with feet and hands.

Here, Jenny does not seem to feel capable of trying to comfort her daughter by means other than the breast, while Anna expresses vividly in her body language her conflicting feelings towards the breast. With her upper body, she is greedily trying to take in as much of the breast as she can while kicking her mother away with her legs and feet. Then she rejects the second breast when it is offered but will again accept the first, yet still struggling and pushing away. This suggests a confusion between good and bad aspects of the breast, perhaps indicative of the kind of excessive splitting and projective identification described earlier.

By the time she was just over a year old Anna was eating solid food in an erratic way but with interest and pleasure. Despite this, Jenny said she had made no progress with weaning. I think it was Jenny's hope that Anna would eventually wean herself when she was "ready". Presumably, a baby would be ready to relinquish the breast when a good object had been internalized that would provide a sufficient inner source of reassurance and security. However, the lack of separateness that continued to a considerable extent to characterize the relationship of this mother and baby would not facilitate the processes of internalization, and this quality of being "mixed up" in each other pervaded all aspects of their life together, even when I observed Anna eating solid food.

In this observation, when Anna was 14 months old, she and her mother were having lunch together:

> Jenny sat opposite Anna and placed the dish on the tray of her highchair. As soon as Jenny lifted her fork to eat, Anna grabbed hard at it and would not let go. Jenny let her keep the fork and picked up Anna's spoon, but Anna pulled Jenny's dish towards herself and tried to pick up the contents with her fork. Jenny soon gave up trying to eat her food and took some of Anna's (wholemeal spaghetti and vegetables). Anna laughed and shouted, banging the fork up and down on the table between mouthfuls.

In this sequence Jenny appears to find it impossible to set limits and to make a boundary between her own meal and Anna's, which results in Anna's omnipotent behaviour. In a similar vein, later in the same observation, Jenny told me that she had removed Anna's cot and placed a small mattress for her on the floor beside her own bed, but Anna did not like this and continued to sleep with Jenny.

An excerpt from the following week's observation illustrates again the confusion surrounding mother's and baby's separate needs for food, which was further exacerbated by Jenny's offering Anna the breast.

> Jenny cut herself a piece of bread. As soon as Anna saw this, she made her way to Jenny, who lifted her up and sat her across her lap. Anna grabbed for the bread and managed to get hold of a corner. Jenny told her she would not like the taste. Anna put it in her mouth and dropped it, still smiling and trying to get some more. Jenny picked up the piece from the floor and quickly popped it into her own mouth, saying "Mmm" and smacking her lips together, laughing. Anna watched Jenny's mouth, smiling uncertainly. She then began to make little whining sounds, which gradually got louder. Her face reddened and she frowned, looking as if she were about to cry. Jenny quickly offered the breast, but Anna did not take the nipple, beginning to cry persistently. Jenny said "What's the matter darling?" in a despairing voice, and Anna writhed and wriggled on her lap but without trying to get down.

It seemed to me that Anna's anger at being offered something other than what she clearly wanted was evident and understandable, but Jenny was unaware that she was eliciting angry feelings towards the breast from Anna.

The difficulties surrounding weaning reached a climax when Anna was about 16 months old. I shall give an excerpt that reveals the fraught nature of the feeding relationship at this time. Here, Anna had been clinging on to Jenny's legs, then fell to the floor when her mother suddenly moved away:

> Jenny sat down and Anna went straight to her, pulling at her jumper. When Jenny lifted Anna onto her lap, Anna pushed her

> away with a strong arm movement and a loud cry, turning away and looking at me. She turned back to Jenny and tried to lift her jumper. Jenny offered the left breast, and Anna took the nipple in her mouth for a few seconds, then turned her head away with a cry. She lifted Jenny's jumper on the other side and did the same. She continued turning from one breast to the other five or six times, apparently frustrated and disgruntled. Jenny said she could not stand this and it could not be nice for Anna either. She said it is perhaps because her milk does not taste good, or that Anna has pain in her mouth from teething or (in a more hopeful voice) perhaps she is weaning. Anna eventually settled for the right breast, fingering the nipple of the left breast as she sucked noisily, wriggling around on Jenny's lap. She seemed to be trying to get her feet to the floor so that she could be standing up and still keep the nipple in her mouth. After a few minutes she turned abruptly away from the breast, got down from Jenny's lap, and made for her toy box.

Here it seemed that for Anna there was little goodness to be found in either breast; both had become so devoid of value that she could not settle for one or the other, and even while her mouth was engaged with the nipple, with the lower half of her body she appeared to be struggling to get away.

Although Jenny voiced her hope that Anna might be ready to wean herself, she seemed to find it difficult to encourage this process by allowing her daughter to endure a measure of frustration. By sometimes refusing to meet Anna's demands, Jenny might have provided both herself and Anna with some relief from the painful and conflicting feelings with which the breast-feeding experience had become imbued. As O'Shaughnessy (1964) points out: "Absence is a natural and essential condition of a relationship, which otherwise becomes a symbiosis detrimental to the separate identify of either person" (pp. 42–43). She emphasizes that a child has an actual need for his object to be absent and that "His own emotional growth will help him oppose the forces which make him cling to the object" (p. 43).

Although the quality of the feeding relationship had become problematic by the time Anna reached the age of 1½ years, no significant change was initiated by either mother or baby. Jenny had become increasingly involved with a group of people who gathered together to play and record music. During a number of my observations at this time, a tape of this music would be playing constantly and Jenny would sit for long periods with her eyes closed, swaying from side to side. Sometimes Anna would lie in her mother's arms, sucking at the breast or gazing into space, seemingly quite affected by the hypnotic quality of the music. At other times she found Jenny's absence of attention unbearable and would do her best to interrupt. Jenny seemed to need to "absent" herself in this way as a means of cutting herself off from Anna, whom she described as "very clinging and demanding". Perhaps Jenny could not tolerate her own infantile aggressive feelings, and in her attempt to "transcend" them they became split off and projected into Anna.

During the latter half of Anna's second year of life, the patterns already described tended to be repeated over and over again. Anna "played" with the breast with frustration rather than pleasure, reaching for the nipple then turning away almost immediately. Her preference for the right breast became more marked, and she usually cried and turned away when Jenny offered the left breast. However, at times both breasts were treated contemptuously, and Anna would turn from one to the other with shouts of discontent and anger.

Before concluding, I shall give one more excerpt from an observation as Anna approached her second birthday. Here, at age 1 year and 10 months, Anna had a heavy cold and was sitting on her mother's lap when I arrived:

> Anna looked at me with recognition but did not smile, her gaze blurred and nose heavily congested. Suddenly she demanded the breast and struggled for access through Jenny's layers of thick clothing, saying "Tit tit tit" in an urgent voice. As soon as Jenny lifted her clothes Anna turned away, then again shouted "Tit tit". This time she sucked for a few seconds, then again turned away.

When I visited Jenny and Anna on an occasional basis during the months following Anna's second birthday, there had been no significant change in the feeding relationship.

I would like to conclude with a few retrospective thoughts about my two years of mother and infant observation. I know little of this mother's early history, and of course it would have been most inappropriate in this context to enquire about Jenny's childhood. However, she often made references to the difficulties that had beset her as a child, as a result of which she felt she had in some way been deprived of good mothering. She told me that she and her sisters had been brought up in an isolated part of Australia by their mother alone, whom Jenny felt had taken a "paternal" role with her children, implying, I think, an absence of closeness and warmth. Jenny often spoke of her mother with disdain or anger, and on the few occasions when I saw them together during mother's visit to this country, there was a sense of distance and lack of contact between mother and daughter. A pointed example of this took place at Anna's first birthday party when Jenny's mother sat away from all the guests in a corner of the room, did not remove her outdoor clothing, and left before the candles on Anna's cake were lit.

Jenny's possible feelings of emotional deprivation and an unconscious identification with a "worthless" mother might help one to understand her need to idealize the breast as a compensation for her own feelings of worthlessness. Moreover, in her rigid adherence to "alternative" beliefs about child-rearing, Jenny may have felt impelled to try to be a different and better sort of mother by providing an idealized breast that allowed for no frustration or pain of separation.

It may be that underlying Jenny's self-admonishments for failing to live up to her expectations of being a perfect mother (she often referred to herself as a "bad mummy") is concealed a phantasy of an internal object that has to be attacked and denigrated. Anna clearly also has angry feelings toward the breast, which her mother is unable to contain and feed back to her in a modified form. Thus it seems likely that through mutual projective identification, mother and daughter collude in a phantasy of attacking the breast.

However, when looking back at my observations with a focus upon Anna, I am struck by the positive aspects of her development, despite the adverse effects upon her arising out of this fraught relationship with the breast. I think it is fair to say that constitutional factors were in her favour. She was from birth a vigorous, energetic, and demanding baby, described by her mother as "quite a little madam who knows what she wants" when just 6 weeks old. She sat, crawled, and walked considerably earlier than the norm, and her capacity for symbolic play and language development did not seem to be impaired.

In his 1985 paper, H. Sydney Klein suggests that "children who are born with much vitality and liveliness themselves are less envious, although more intolerant of frustration" (p. 35). It could have been the case for Anna that had she been endowed with a preponderance of envy, her early personality development might have been severely impoverished by phantasied attacks on an object presented by mother as so relentlessly perfect.

However, it did not seem particularly to be Anna's envy of the breast that destroyed for her its goodness, but, rather, a complex process whereby her mother's idealization concealed and compensated for the damaged state of her own internal object. The primitive need to project unwanted parts of the personality into a suitable container would be met for Jenny in the birth of her own child, who could then function as that part of her self which needs continually to attack its object. This would, in effect, make it extremely difficult for Jenny to acknowledge Anna as being separate from herself.

H. Sydney Klein (1985) notes that "The effect of the mother's anxieties on the child's capacity to develop is often shown in those cases in which the mother, instead of being able to act as a container for the child's feelings and anxieties, uses the child instead as a container for her own" (p. 38). Perhaps also Anna had to turn the breast into an object of contempt as her only means of refusing to take in all her mother's feelings and anxieties.

In a paper delivered in 1984 at the Tavistock Clinic, London, Livia di Cagno drew attention to the factor of liveliness in babies as being highly significant in the establishment of a good mother–infant relationship. To quote from her study of three problematic cases: "It is so possible that negative elements can be counteracted, if the positive ones prevail. We could mention an element which was common to these three cases . . . which was the vitality of these babies."

Hopefully, for this mother and baby, the positive developmental impetus springing from Anna's lively nature might to some extent serve to mitigate the negative effects of Jenny's difficulties in relating to her baby as a whole and separate person. On the other hand, if Anna has come to treat the breast with contempt, it may be that she will internalize and become identified with a devalued object, engendering feelings of maternal inadequacy in her adult life.

On returning to my feelings of sadness and irony that I described at the beginning, it seems to me that Jenny's attempt to prolong endlessly the very special intimacy of the early feeding relationship, and indeed of the pre-birth period, was doomed to failure. The outcome of this mother's efforts to avoid for herself and Anna the frustrations and pain of separation was that the idealized breast became an object fraught with conflicting feelings for her baby.

CHAPTER TWO

Feeding difficulties in infancy: Faruk and Shereen

Mariângela Mendes de Almeida Pinheiro

Two cases of early feeding difficulties are presented in this chapter. I intend to discuss some conditions in which early feeding problems, variations in appetite, or decreased emotional availability for feeding seem to escalate into an anti-growth cycle within the parent–infant relationship. As in a vicious circle, such feeding problems may evoke massive parental anxiety, interfering significantly with the quality of the feeding experience. This may even lead to persistent food refusal by the infant, which, in turn, intensifies parental despair.

Faruk and Shereen were seen at the Child and Adolescent Psychiatry Department, North Middlesex Hospital, London, where I worked as a psychologist. These infants and their parents were referred by the Paediatric Department and seen as part of a clinical study investigating factors of risk and resilience with six infants aged from 0 to 18 months presenting feeding problems. According to paediatric reports available to me prior to the beginning of my work with these families, no organic cause had been found to account for their difficulties.

Psychoanalytic infant observation was used as a basic tool for understanding the relationships involved and the presenting problem. Observational skills developed from infant observation training were complemented and integrated into a clinical intervention approach, in a format better defined as "participant observation", where I shared perceptions with the parents as an attempt to strengthen parent–infant communication and parental responsiveness towards the infant. My contact with the parents and babies as outpatients (or, alternatively, in the hospital paediatric ward) and in a home visit included sharing perceptions of the infant's play and feeding situations within the family context. Parents' concerns, anxieties, and potentialities for attunement with their infant's needs were explored, taking into account the presented feeding difficulties.

For the presentation of the cases in this chapter, I shall concentrate on the exploration of the problems and work carried out only during the clinical study.

Faruk:
humouring mother/resisting depressed states

Faruk was referred at the age of 10 months, with his food refusal causing great worry to his parents, mainly his mother. There was no immediate medical concern with Faruk's physical health, and he looked bright and alert. He had presented oesophageal reflux (involuntary regurgitation of the stomach contents into the mouth and oesophagus), treated successfully with medication by the paediatrician.

Faruk was the only son of a young refugee couple from a famine-stricken country, who were going through stresses in their relationship and in fact became separated when Faruk was approximately 1 year and 3 months old.

Faruk's feeding problems had begun when he was starting to be bottle-fed, around the age of 3 months. From age 3 to 6 months he used to vomit, and when solid foods were introduced, he did not accept them easily. His parents had developed strategies of distracting Faruk while feeding him, or giving him the bottle when he was asleep. "Otherwise," they said, "he would refuse to eat. He is not interested in food." They felt that his attention needed to be taken away from the food, so that he could "swallow without noticing it". Pleasure and enjoyment seemed to be completely absent in the feeding interaction.

In that context, Faruk seemed to lack awareness of the distinctive complementary roles in a feeding situation, having little sense of a parental object who feeds and with whom he can firmly connect. This was demonstrated in our first appointment in the hospital, when I saw him with both parents:

> Faruk came closer to the bag where there was some food. Mother picked up the milk bottle from the bag to feed him. She held the bottle in his mouth, with Faruk standing up straight in front of her, not touching her or the bottle. He remained in that relatively passive posture (which made me think of him being fed while lying down asleep), with his arms down alongside his body, sucking the bottle for a while. I asked the parents how he eats or drinks and whether he sometimes holds the bottle. Mother then let him hold the bottle and he did that for some seconds, but he did not keep the necessary inclination for the juice to come into his mouth. He also seemed a little distractible and not very clear as to where he should put his hands. The bottle soon fell to the floor. He seemed to have lost interest in feeding. Mother picked up the bottle and kept it. I commented that Faruk seemed to be exploring what he needs to do and what others need to do to get the feeding going.

Faruk's way of not accepting food presented itself initially through vomiting, and then through dribbling. Like his limp holding and dropping of the bottle in the example above, Faruk's vomiting and dribbling seemed to be an enactment of his difficulties in containing within himself what he had taken in without noticing. The food, introduced while he was distracted or asleep, was returned or leaked out as if it was not held firmly inside.

When Faruk was 1 year and 4 months, he started to shake his head and close his mouth to refuse food. This seemed to provide a different way of resisting what he seemed to perceive as an intrusion rather than a facilitating response to his needs. In a situation in which he had little experience of attuned parental regulation or self-regulation of his nourishment needs, Faruk may have channelled his efforts at regulatory competence into avoiding or refusing the feeding experience. Maybe he was trying to rescue some kind of agency or sense of self-discrimination in the nutritional exchange with his environment, which was usually an experience cloaked in sleep or distraction.

Besides, perhaps feeling more alive himself through his attempts at regulation, including hypothetically his feed refusal, Faruk's sense of parents as lively or vital objects seemed to depend on his parents' reactions and concerns towards his avoidance or refusal of food.

Faruk's parents, stressed by social isolation and family tensions, appeared to be "struggling to thrive" socially and emotionally, with very limited support. The context back home was of war, crisis, hunger, deprivation, and fragmentation of bonds due to people having to move from village to village after food. Mother was even more prone to depressed moods, since she had left the home country on her own and had no way of knowing whether her relatives were still alive. In that context, there was very little space in Mother's mind for containment of Faruk's distresses, understanding of little upsets, and "enlivening" (Alvarez, 1992) of their relationship.

In a home visit when Faruk was 1 year and 4 months, Mother looked even more sad and upset than usual. She explained that her husband had left her a month previously and was now living with his mother, who had never accepted her son's marriage and would have preferred him to have married another woman. "He likes his mother, so he went." Father kept visiting Faruk, but sometimes spent weeks without coming. Mother noticed that Faruk sometimes seemed to look for Father by wandering around in the flat. His feeding problem, which had improved slightly with the sessions ("Faruk was eating what he liked"), was concerning her again: "We are back to the same problems; for a month he hasn't been eating well. I try everything but he shakes his head, he is not eating anything again." Mother reported that when Father came to play briefly with Faruk in fortnightly visits, the child looked happy and ate very well on those days. She seemed aware that Faruk's mood interfered with his eating. On that occasion, she also commented in a resentful and sad way how she had felt very little support from her husband's relatives since Faruk was born:

> She talked about having been very ill after his birth. It was a difficult and long labour by forceps. After twenty-five days she started to bleed, and that went on for four months. She described this as "her period not stopping", also implying that some damage had been done to her by the forceps. She still feels pain in her lower abdomen, which she connects with the labour. She talked about her husband's relatives not helping her when she was back from labour and was staying in their house for several days. She had not imagined that when she had a baby she would have so little support from relatives, because in their culture people help each other very much when they have babies. We talked about Mother's feelings of anger and helplessness around that difficult start with Faruk.

As she felt isolated and sad, with little support from friends or relatives, Mother herself would not bother to eat sometimes and was reluctant to go out with Faruk. Feeding times albeit distressing, seemed to be the main remaining moments in which an active level of interaction would take place. As seen through Mother's eyes when Faruk was 1 year and 5 months:

> Mother became tearful when we talked about her and Faruk being on their own. She talked about them being the most important thing for each other. Faruk, who was around Mother's chair, exploring the space in the corner of the room, at this moment came closer to Mother and stood near her, with both hands on her knees, producing a timid laugh and looking at her. "He cheers me up," she said. We talked about how sometimes it may be difficult for Faruk to see his mother sad. I commented that Faruk perhaps perceives her struggle to feed him as a sign of her being more active and lively. Mother said that she keeps all her energy for Faruk, and she is really happy when he eats—she tries everything to see that happening.

The value of food and feeding for Mother was naturally intensely coloured by the background of starvation that involved her relatives in her homeland. Perhaps she felt guilty for having food here while her family could be dying there. She felt anger and bewilderment towards Faruk's refusal of such a vital, precious, and not always available source of life. Mother's depressed mood could also be sensed in the way she seemed to undervalue her own capacity to physically and emotionally nourish Faruk. It was as if she felt Faruk was rejecting not only her food, but also her words and her capacity to have an impact on him. This was illustrated in another vignette from the same session quoted above:

> Faruk was very active in the middle of the room picking toys up from the box. When he was throwing a brick on the floor, Mother looked at him and firmly but gently called him and gestured "No" with her hand. Faruk looked very attentively to Mother and immediately put the brick gently in the box. I commented on how he seemed to listen to her very keenly. She said that he listens more to his father. She commented that it was Father who used to tell him "not to do this, not to do that" and Faruk listens to his father. "If I say something to Faruk he doesn't listen," she added. I commented that he seemed to have listened to her quite well here. She smiled and commented that she does not tell Faruk off very often about things he can't do. "He is small, he is a baby, he can do anything that he likes. . . . It was his father who used to tell him what things he shouldn't do," she said. We talked about how she is feeling on her own and how she feels it is difficult to cope with Faruk's needs without her husband.

Faruk appeared to sense his mother's depressed moods and deprivation, and he alternated between moments of cheering her up in an engaging way and moments of defensive avoidance and self-sufficiency. At times when she was force-feeding him or struggling with him over food, she thought with relief of the time when he would soon be able to eat with his own hands.

The following extract is from a home visit when Faruk was 1 year and 4 months, a month after Father had left. It gives us some indication of Faruk's feeling that he somehow needed to provide something for a desired but possibly depleted, deprived object before he could ask anything from it:

> When I was picking up the diary from my handbag to make the next appointment, Faruk looked very curious and came closer,

> trying to get the pencil I was writing with. Mother gave him a toy (a metal car) instead. He threw it energetically on the floor. She gave him another car, and he threw it away as well. I gave Mother the pencil and wondered whether she would like to give it to him for a moment just to see what would happen. He accepted the pencil from Mother and cried when it had to be returned to me. He then gave me a car and looked at me with expectation, still crying. Mother laughed, saying that he wanted to exchange one for the other (the car for the pencil). He picked up another car and gave it to me. He then started very purposefully, while crying and sobbing, to pick up the toys on the floor one by one and to put all of them on my lap, until it was full. He continued to cry in a touching way, and I wondered to myself why he seemed to feel that someone needed to be offered so many things to give him what he wanted. Did this relate to a precept of a needy mother?

The tendency of some children of depressed mothers to find themselves mothering their mothers has been mentioned in the literature (Raphael-Leff, 1991). Precocious responsibility and often brittle maturity may be fostered in these children. Perhaps Faruk's cheering-up of his mother, and his tendency to self-sufficiency, were early signs of that trend in his development.

Faruk's feeding difficulties improved, albeit with some oscillations. The difficulties in the family persisted, and this had an impact on Mother's depressed moods and breadth of their social life.

Shereen: the long-lasting object/ under the impact of massive primitive projections

Shereen was a small, delicate, passive, and accommodating baby. She was referred to our department at age 5 months because of her failure to thrive. She refused food, mainly solids. In the paediatric clinic, Shereen had received successful treatment with medication for her gastro-oesophageal reflux, but the poor feeding, lack of weight gain, and inadequate growth continued.

Shereen's mother was a single parent with two older daughters (8 and 4 years old) from a previous partner. Shereen was an unwanted child. Mother described Shereen as a frightened, "nervy" baby. This is an extract of our first meeting, when Shereen was 6 months old:

> With Shereen nestled on her lap, Mother commented, with a grimacing face, that Shereen is a jumpy baby, different from her other children. "She is frightened of noises in the street, of deep voices or any other noise. Even with routine noises in the house like the Hoover, she gets unsettled. She gets tense and clingy in these situations." Mother linked it with herself not being calm during the pregnancy, thinking that Shereen would be different if the pregnancy had been better. She added that Shereen's main problem was with food: "She isn't interested in food at all." Mother felt that Shereen did something to reject the food, to put it out. "Sometimes she looks as if she is going to take the food, but somehow she manages not to have. . . . I have tried everything, all possible nice things, she does not even take them to her mouth. . . ." During this meeting Shereen struck me as a very quiet baby, who moved her body very little, although her eyes seemed to look around with interest. When Mother moved her to sit on the floor near her legs, she remained quiet, giving me the impression that she would stay where she was put.

Mother knew before Shereen was born that she would not have any help from the child's father. He had said that if the baby got sick, he would give no support. He would not have anything to do with the baby. She had thought about abortion, and in the beginning of the pregnancy had not eaten well, imagining that not eating would be an acceptable, less guilt-provoking way of naturally inducing termination of pregnancy: "If Nature took it, it wouldn't be so bad." In spite of ambivalent thoughts, conflicting suggestions, and intense anxiety, Mother decided to keep the baby. During pregnancy she used to have the feeling that her baby was going to need hospital assistance, because she herself was so tense and distressed, crying all the time. She feared that her state of mind might have an influence on the baby.

After Shereen's birth, Mother felt very depressed and was initially poorly attached to the baby. Her impression that something was wrong with Shereen started from the second day after birth: "She used to get tired, exhausted when at the breast." Shereen was breast-fed for three weeks, then Mother interrupted it because Shereen was vomiting. She felt that Shereen was not interested in feeding from her breast. Mother felt more comfortable with the bottle: "I could see that she was taking the milk and could check how much."

Mother experienced Shereen's early feeding problems, her poor, picky eating habits, as a punishment directed at her for not having wanted the baby and for not eating well during the beginning of the pregnancy. Mother's interpretation of Shereen's relationship with the breast as a retaliatory refusal interfered with her capacity to explore Shereen's behaviour as fresh communications, and to respond to it with a containing, receptive attitude, which could help both of them to find ways of dealing with this new experience. Mother still felt for many months that, by not feeding well, and being very selective, Shereen was telling her that "everything was horrible", that "she was not interested in anything".

Mother perceived Shereen's difficulties as rejecting and attacking of herself as a projection of her own feelings now lodged in Shereen. Mother therefore tended to see the child's picky attitude and reluctance to feed in the light of her own selective responses to unwanted indigestible experiences. In this context, Shereen could be struggling to digest not only food, but also negative maternal projections, of which she was being a receptacle. In an active exercise of selecting and regulating her feeding, Shereen could be trying to maintain some filtering and discriminating capacity in the face of the mixed and intrusive quality of Mother's communications accompanying the actual food.

At our first meeting, Mother talked about Shereen's determination and pickiness:

> Mother explained that Shereen coughs when not wanting more food. "Coughing is her sign that if you insist, she will vomit." On the floor near Mother's legs, Shereen looked a bit unsettled, crying, and Mother took it as indication that she wanted milk.

> Mother responded quickly, getting the bottle, and Shereen started to drink it eagerly. I pointed out her eagerness. Mother commented that it was better now with the medication. She also added that Shereen takes only milk in the bottle; the juice has to be put in another container, otherwise she does not take it. "She puzzles me!" Mother observed. We talked about how Mother seemed to see Shereen as very selective and determined about what she wanted and how she wanted to take things in. I wondered to myself whether this lessened Mother's doubts about the worth of what she had to offer to Shereen.

By the time Shereen was referred, she was only accepting liquids. Any solid food was spat out. During our second contact, when Shereen was 6 months old, Mother expressed her frustration:

> "I have tried everything to get her interested in other foods, but she doesn't even swallow it, doesn't even taste it. I give her nice things, not bitter tastes, but she doesn't take anything. She is not even trying." I commented that Mother might be feeling rejected by that, after all her effort to give Shereen something good and nourishing.
>
> During this conversation Shereen played by throwing away and retrieving a toy and a soft cube that I had offered to her from the box of toys.

Later in this session, Mother and Shereen related to one another as if in an early feeding situation, with Mother feeling unsure initially of what she would be offering to her "demanding" baby, but then apparently reassuring herself when the child welcomed her offer:

> Shereen, sitting on Mother's lap, seemed a bit unsettled now, wriggling her body and stretching her arms alongside her body and backwards, sometimes turning her body towards Mother's big plastic handbag on the floor. I asked what she might be wanting, and Mother said it was the bottle. Mother was doubtful about whether to give it to Shereen or not, because it might have gone cold and "Shereen only likes it when it's warm". Mother got the bottle and, feeling it was still a bit warm,

decided to give it to the baby. In Mother's arms, Shereen started to suck promptly and eagerly, touching Mother's fingers and then moving her arm towards Mother's neck and holding it. I mentioned that Shereen seemed very much to create the atmosphere of a breast-feeding situation, taking milk from the bottle as if from the breast, only liking it warm as if just from the breast. After a little while, Shereen seemed to have got enough from the bottle and started to move her legs and arms, making continuous sounds and grimaces, looking upset again. Mother commented that sometimes she wants her pacifier. Mother gave it to her, and she started to suck it vigorously, calming herself down.

In her avoidance of solids, Shereen seemed to be protecting herself from what was felt as an uncomfortable external intrusion, refusing "lumps" that she might feel were very difficult to chew, swallow, digest, and metabolize. She preferred to take in soft, smooth, liquids or lick something long-lasting like lollipops, which would not vanish and leave her unsatisfied. They also did not require her to be actively biting and aggressive. She seemed to be avoiding such "devouring" aspects, which were perhaps linked to pluralities evoked by her abrupt weaning.

Around 7 months old, Shereen was admitted to the hospital paediatric ward for three days with wheezing. Within two weeks, she was hospitalized again for two days and was diagnosed asthmatic. According to Mother, the asthma episodes were usually preceded by Shereen's vomiting. Mother tried to stay with Shereen in hospital most of the time. One of our sessions took place in the paediatric ward, during the second hospitalization:

Mother said that she was a bit shocked when she saw Shereen with all the instruments in hospital (meters, oxygen mask, etc.), because she imagined that that meant that she was in quite a bad state. She associated the diagnosis of asthma with Shereen's father's side of the family, as a paternal uncle had had asthma. Mother said that Shereen has been well, apart from the wheezing. Her feeding problem has been better, and she is now starting to try to eat peaches. Mother is happy that she is showing interest in other foods besides milk.

> Shereen looked exhausted on Mother's lap, mainly sleeping for most of the time. Sometimes she opened her eyes very slowly, as if weakened by her condition. Sometimes she seemed to try to get rid of the oxygen mask, moving her head jerkily, and moaning as if irritated and unsettled. When doctors came to collect blood for examination and took her fist for the "injection", she cried out loud as if wanting to expel something bad from her. Mother seemed to cope quite calmly with Shereen's distress, accommodating her warmly on her lap and talking to her. Mother commented that Shereen was now losing weight. We talked about how that might be more connected to the general fragility rather than to the eating.
>
> When having the injection, Shereen jerked around, with bouts of tense crying. Her sisters came along to be with her, and they were concerned about her loud and desperate cries. Shereen calmed down and allowed herself to be held by her mother when the injection was over. She still looked sleepy and tired.

For a child like Shereen for whom protection from external "entries" was so essential, we can imagine that the hospitalization, the medical instruments, and the injections must have felt overwhelmingly intrusive or invasive. It was interesting to see, however, that in a situation where Mother sees herself as guilt-free, and even personally supported, she is more available to comfort Shereen.

Shereen soon went home, and during the rest of the time we worked together (until she was approximately 2 years old) no other significant hospitalization was reported, although Shereen was still prone to colds.

Food and feeding seemed to be intense issues for both Shereen and her mother. These issues signalled internal states and were perceived as crudely controlling life and death. Mother reported her own unwillingness to eat when going through any problems and had, in fact, stopped eating during her pregnancy, with the belief that she would then abort the baby. Similarly, Shereen's health upsets, like colds and wheezing problems, were, according to Mother, always preceded by episodes of vomiting: "This is the first sign Shereen gives me when something is not going well. This is her way of letting me know that there's something wrong." We see here how Shereen's conflicting needs expressed themselves through extreme and desperate ejecting defences. We can also speculate that Mother may have missed or misperceived Shereen's more subtle cues. She focused on rejecting and expulsive behaviour such as vomiting. Would Mother have been more available for attunement if Shereen could have used less extreme behaviour? She seemed to be so wrapped up in her own preoccupations and guilt that she had perhaps little space for an attentive and unhurried exploration of Shereen's subtler and sometimes tentative signs.

Mother described Shereen as "doing something to her food, like coughing and making herself sick". She commented in despair, when Shereen was 6 months old: "If Shereen was not a baby she would be called an anorexic, refusing food, vomiting, making herself sick." Perhaps Shereen needed to feel that she could control the flow of nourishment herself, which was not the case at the time of her abrupt weaning, which was a painful experience of rupture and loss.

As Mother said, Shereen (when 7 months old) had started to chew peaches and to suck lollipops, still feeling more comfortable with chewing things that lasted longer, things she could almost suck, since she was not yet confident in taking in or swallowing any "lumps". We talked at that time about Shereen's way of taking something in cautiously and, little by little, controlling carefully how much she was taking in, but also how much still remained. She seemed to hold on to what could be felt as securely available—like a tightly controlled transitional object.

The fear, apparently shared by Mother and Shereen, of something destructive acquired a new and painful light when I learnt in one of our meetings that Mother had lost her own mother when she was 9 months old. She described that time of her life as "when I was Shereen's age". She did not know the cause of her mother's death, and she had been placed in a children's home and had no subsequent contact with her father. Now she wanted to trace her past and know more about her parents, but she was "worried about digging it up". For Shereen's mother, that seemed to be an indigestible "lump of reality" that she tried to avoid "chewing". Like

Shereen, she might have had fears about the omnipotence of her infantile destructiveness, which was then intensely reactivated during her undesired pregnancy.

At times, Shereen and her mother both seemed to be trapped in mutual depression and indigestible projections, both of them unable to attract each other's liveliness, in a vicious cycle of hopelessness. Shereen's awareness of her mother's needs and deprivation seemed to be expressed in the sequence reported by her mother at 13 months, when Shereen would sometimes feed Mother instead of taking the food herself.

The most important area of work in my contact with Shereen and her mother was helping Mother to discriminate between Shereen's internal world and her own. This was reflected in her comment when I asked her about how she felt about the sessions:

> "It helps me to think that I am not completely responsible for the problem Shereen is having, that she is herself a little person. . . . Sometimes I can see that she is taking her time."

Shereen seemed to have failed to mobilize Mother's "aliveness" towards her, which would have stimulated her to be alive to what Mother and the environment could offer her. Shereen's limited relation with her environment was shown in this extract from an outpatient session, when Shereen was 10 months old:

> Mother initially sat with Shereen on her lap, started talking, and then put the child in the centre of the room, facing the toy box, her back to Mother. Shereen related to the box very timidly, sometimes even looking a little afraid of touching or exploring the toys more fully. Most of the time she held a brick tightly, moving it with her hand while sitting by the box. She maintained eye contact with me, sometimes looked relaxed and smiled, but moved very little and seldom explored the toys.

In this meeting, Mother put me in touch with her anxiety about taking things in. This evoked in my countertransference feelings of being, at times, gently nourishing and at times intrusively force-feeding.

> Mother commented that friends and people around her kept suggesting things for her to do and things for her to prepare for Shereen. However, nothing worked, and she felt the comments as an overload. I said that that was similar to how she felt during her pregnancy, with other people giving different opinions and commenting on what she should do. She said that if someone comes up and suggests something, she tells them to try that themselves, because she has tried everything and nothing has worked. I commented that she seemed to feel rather lost when confronted with so many suggestions. Mother seemed to be touched emotionally by something in that comment, starting to cry quietly, exposing some fragility and vulnerability that she seemed to have been trying to avoid previously in other sessions.

As we continued talking, Mother seemed to feel freer to relate to Shereen from a different perspective, perhaps because she felt contained and could get in touch with her pain and less in need of projecting it. Shereen's apparently passive and non-demanding nature presented then a different facet. She was seen as "alive" and "enlivening", rather than as a projection of Mother's aggression or as a damaged result of Mother's rejection. In the continuation of the session quoted above, Shereen's capacity to change in response to maternal shifts is observable, for example, when Mother alerts her, arouses her, or "reclaims her" (Alvarez, 1992).

> Shereen seemed to me very undemanding while I was talking to Mother. She entertained herself with just a wooden brick, which she held tightly. From time to time, she looked at me in front of her.
>
> I commented that the way Shereen was playing was similar to what Mother described as typical of her feeding (e.g. eating very little, limited selection of food, not showing "hunger"). We started to talk about Shereen's play and playful moments, trying to explore Mother's involvement with her in those situations. Mother said that Shereen liked to play quietly in her own space, and I wondered aloud with Mother whether Shereen,

even when she appears content, might welcome and enjoy Mother's attempts to play with her.

Mother came closer to Shereen, redirecting her face towards the child and changing her own position in the chair a little, as if allowing herself a new perspective. Shereen then engaged in continuous eye contact with Mother while playing and exchanging with her the brick that she had held continuously and tightly in her hand. For the first time in the meeting, Shereen actively kept contact and, from that moment onwards, did not stop looking at Mother, moving towards her, giving her toys, moving her arms and face in a more expressive and lively way. It appeared that, given the opportunity, she would respond much more actively and show more interest in contact, toys, and perhaps food. I pointed out to Mother the difference in Shereen since Mother had started to direct herself towards the child and play with her. Although Mother seemed to agree, I alternated between feeling useful and supportive and feeling intrusive, like the people she had referred to who commented on what she should do to help Shereen.

Shereen continued to seek Mother through gestures, looks, and smiles. We talked about how eager Shereen seemed to be to play with Mother and how she was now more interested in different toys from the box. I commented on how Mother's more active engagement with Shereen had made it easier for the child to explore objects that she had not been interested in exploring before.

Here we have a hint of Mother's capacity for receptive and enlivening containment. Shereen responds to it by perceiving her as a less frightened and less frightening object (i.e. a live object, surviving destructive projections). For Shereen, the enlivening and enlivened Mother could also be reassuring inasmuch as she felt that aggressive projections could be dealt with. When they managed to play, Shereen's involvement with the same hard toy in a monotonous and lifeless way was replaced by a livelier exploration of different toys. Through play and emotional contact with Mother, Shereen became able to "let go", to relinquish the tight hold on the hard solid object and perhaps begin to develop a sense of a long-lasting, trustable object within herself. That seemed to open up the possibility of change in Shereen's reluctance to take in different kinds of food. If supported by consistent, repeated experiences of containment with Mother, she could probably move on to new explorations.

During two years of work with this mother and child, I could see them struggling to build up a livelier relationship. I could see the child very slowly showing more interest in eating food and "tasting" the environment (the sisters were a substantial support). Each new developmental step, however—for example, potty-training or starting nursery—was permeated by intense maternal projections and difficulties in considering the child's signs and pace. Mother and child alternated between periods of enjoying little progress and phases of depression and hopelessness in Mother. These feelings were part (but only part) of the relationship with Shereen, and they deserved special attention. As a continuation of our work, a referral of individual psychotherapy for Mother was made.

Discussion and conclusion

When working with parents and infants like Faruk and Shereen, we can see how the way they relate to food is paralleled by modes of containing, digesting, and processing emotional content within the relationship. Difficulties in metabolizing actual food—illustrated here through Faruk and Shereen's vomiting, food refusal, spitting, difficulties in swallowing, and avoidance of solids—seem to correspond to difficulties in mentally "digesting" emotional experiences, as expressed by their parents and observed in the parent–infant relationship.

We can see how, from very early in life, an infant is in contact with his parent's ways of dealing with psychic pain and anxiety. The infant perceives the parents' preferred (or available) modes of processing emotional experiences. We can see here the parents struggling to cope with, digest, and metabolize psychic pain, and this fosters learning through experience (Bion, 1962), but many times we see them resorting to getting rid of their pain through denial and projection. Anxiety was usually evaded and pushed away, rather than contained and modulated. The support from what I have come to call a "containing field"—that is, a network of containing relationships where infantile and painful aspects can be receptively held—was inconsistent within these families. Within this context, flaws in the parental containing capacities interfere with the infant's capacity to process emotional experience, and this results in psychic tension that may also have an impact on the infant's capacity to take in and digest actual food.

Factors of vulnerability or of resilience in the child, in the family, and in the supporting environment increase or decrease the risks of persistence in these cases of feeding problems. I shall discuss these factors in detail.

Pre- and perinatal difficulties such as conflicted pregnancies, complicated labours, and postpartum experiences (not supported by a containing surrounding environment) were part of the history of these cases. From very early on, the exchanges between mothers and babies were characterized by fantasies of the baby draining maternal resources or taking control over them, and sometimes by maternal feelings of internal damage by the baby or by the labour that engendered conscious or unconscious hostile feelings towards the newborn or the pregnancy . Feelings of guilt were present. The baby's variations of appetite, pace of feeding, or early difficulties at the breast were often experienced as reproach and retaliation towards the mother.

When mothers were rather depressed and tended to self-devaluation, they saw the feeding problems as persecutory and totally their fault. Shereen's mother perceived her daughter's early feeding difficulties as evidence of an absolute lack of interest in her or even as evidence of blame. We saw how easily she tended to focus on the child's major expressions of discomfort rather than on her less extreme manifestations.

For these infants, the capacity to recognize and signal their internal states of need, such as hunger, might well have been diminished in a context of parental unavailability to receive, explore, and attempt to understand the meaning of their cues. When a more receptive mode of containment was provided by the mother for the infant (and by the observer for the mother)—for example, as shown in Shereen's last vignettes—the infant's signals were more readily noticed by the parents, probably facilitating the infant's capacity to express him/herself with greater clarity.

Though maternal depressed moods often interfere with containing abilities and affect an infant's feeding and other aspects of his or her development, we have to take into account that responsive and lively babies have greater chances of helping their mothers out of their depression. Thus, while Shereen seemed to have little capacity to withstand the intensity of her mother's hopelessness, Faruk seemed to challenge his mother's depression by showing that he was alive and so was she. He was therefore more prepared to make use of the slightest sign of life available from his mother and was himself more able to contribute to her feeling more vital.

Unmourned losses and imminence of loss of relatives were also part of the history of the cases here described. These losses were either kept at bay or incompletely mourned. However, a terror of death was powerfully reawakened in the parents by their child not eating or losing weight. They seemed to be facing, then, not only the threat of a new loss, but also the revival of earlier unmetabolized guilt feelings, impotence, and possible doubts about their own destructive impulses. This was particularly intense in Shereen's case. When the anxiety about the survival of the child was associated with actual catastrophic experiences (the famine in Faruk's parents' home country), the perception of the child's communication seemed to be less distorted than when the fears were primarily determined by internal phantasies (Shereen's case).

With parental projections being massive and intrusive, the parents' capacity to relate to the actual child was impaired. The parents seemed to easily miss the real infant's cues for pacing, amount, and duration of feeding. Patterns of feeding in the families studied included coaxing, force-feeding, tense and anxious feeding, feeding while the baby was asleep or distracted, and feeding without attention to the infant's signs and needs for a break. Meal times, when not dispersed and evaded, were a battleground.

Food was sometimes offered as an immediate response when the infant expressed any kind of distress. In this sense, food was not accompanied by a containing attitude, which explored and decoded the infant's signs. On the contrary, it was a contradictory offer of non-availability, a buffer for anxiety. Parents were prompted to action, offering food as the "great pacifier", not only because of the child's distress, but also because of their own anxieties, which they found harder to contain and think about. A model of avoidance and evacuation rather than containment—of "action" rather than thought—was offered, to be internalized by the infant. This difficulty of "mental containment and digestion" was possibly reflected in the infant's feeding problem, as the infant struggled to metabolize not only the food offered, but also the parents' evacuating modes of dealing with experience.

The persistence of Faruk's and Shereen's difficulties were certainly influenced by the lack of outside support for their mothers, making it more difficult for the cycle of depression and parental self-depreciation to be interrupted. Irritability, self-sufficiency when playing on their own, over-selectiveness, and a tendency to withdrawal or detachment were common features observed in these infants. These features, combined with the difficulties in taking in the nourishment, make us wonder about parallels between eating disorders in infants and in adults, especially the reluctance to allow dependency on one's objects and the need to exert control over impulses and objects (Palazzoli, 1963). The wish to be in control of feelings and internal states may well be displaced to the need to be in control of food supplies (Reiser, 1990).

The shutting of the mouth to food and taking things in, in a wider sense, seems to be a variety of what Gianna Williams refers to as the "no-entry" syndrome. These babies were not only confronted with a parental object often unable to contain their projections, but they were themselves in many cases receptacles of parental projections. The deep anxiety they may experience about anything (including food) "getting inside" them seems connected to a need to preserve themselves from what is experienced by them as a threatening intrusion. In this context, food may be a source of great anxiety (Williams, 1997).

Different degrees of resilience in these infants seemed to determine the impact of the actual baby on the transformation of parental phantasies and mental representations. Children vary in their tolerance and disposition and in their response to parental projections. This can at times be transformed, modulated, or appeased or at other times can grow and be magnified. The babies seemed to show different capacities to filter massive projections, before succumbing to them, giving in to collapse, or before having to build a rigid, impairing system of defence. Shereen, for example, seemed to have had few opportunities to transform and reduce the intensity of her mother's sense of guilt and fear of having damaged her child from very early on in her development.

The establishment of anti-growth cycles of relationship for these infants and their parents seemed, therefore, to depend mainly on the intensity, content, quality, and permeability of parental projections on individual capacities to metabolize pain and accept dependency, and on the level and type of containment of infantile aspects available in the family and surrounding network.

In Shereen's case, the main complicating factors seemed to be unmourned losses, guilt for hostile feelings, and conflictual pregnancy, with a high level of projections taking place probably even before the infant's birth. To this we must add: abrupt weaning, lack of close support from a "containing field", devaluation of the maternal figure, maternal depressed moods, food offered as response to distress, lack of resilience in the child with a passive tendency to withdraw, and parental tendency to encourage the child's self-sufficiency.

With Faruk, there were also a large number of factors contributing to the establishment of his feeding problems: a difficult start in life, maternal depression and consequent non-containing modes of relationship, excessive parental projections interfering with devaluation of mothering, tension in family relationships, flat and inaccurate perception of the infant's signs and communications, and the infant's tendency to self-sufficiency (fostered by the mother). However, in his case we could see some mitigating factors, including the infant's resilience and capacity for enlivenment of the relationship with his mother and the different quality of projections (the fears were linked to real threat), and these had significant impact preventing an anti-growth cycle from becoming intensely crystallized.

Feeding problems are a common reason for hospital admissions or referrals to a paediatrician in early infancy. Families undergoing the stress of struggling with a non-organic feeding problem seem to be more effectively helped in the long run when these difficulties are seen in the context of their relationship. Indeed, we have seen here how problems in early feeding may be connected with difficulties in processing emotional experiences, which resonate in other areas of development and psychological growth of the infant. Early parent–infant intervention is, therefore, a valuable instrument in supporting individual and interactive resilience factors, benign channels of parent–infant interchanges, and growth-promoting cycles of relationship.

CHAPTER THREE

Getting to know Miral: some thoughts on the nature of feeding difficulties in the psychotherapy of a 5-year-old boy

Selina Perocevic

In this chapter, I describe my work with Miral, a boy with feeding and other difficulties that had led different professionals to think at various points in time that his development was retarded, or that he had autistic features, or, more recently, that he had Asperger's syndrome. I shall highlight relevant themes from the once-weekly psychotherapy spanning two years and extract from his complex and fragmented clinical presentation aspects that could throw some light on his long-standing difficulties with taking in food and internalizing experiences.

Miral arrived, without a formal diagnosis, at the Child and Adolescent Mental Health Service where I work, the referring psychologist having asked our clinic to help with his emotional and social immaturity. As I got to know Miral, I thought that he was a child troubled by autistic anxieties who seemed to live in and out of psychotic states (Rustin, Rhode, Dubinsky, & Dubinsky, 1997), and whose pathology had similarities with adult borderline states (Steiner, 1993).

I first saw this boy one month before his fifth birthday. Having met his parents, I saw Miral on his own five times at weekly intervals. During this assessment period, both his school and his parents reported major improvements in Miral's interactions with others and his appetite for food. I then offered to see him for therapy once a week, as an offer of intensive work that I had thought to be more appropriate was not available at our clinic. There were important family issues that a colleague and I hoped to address through family sessions, before starting to see Miral for individual psychotherapy. Unfortunately, the family work was short lived, due both to the parents' lack of interest in it and to the rapid worsening of Miral's symptoms by the end of his individual assessment sessions. We first met two years ago, and I have now been seeing Miral for psychotherapy for just over a year and a half. Our work will come to an end in a few months' time, due to my planned departure from the clinic. Miral will then be 7½ years old. I hope to arrange for another child psychotherapist to work with Miral after I leave, as I think that this child has benefited greatly from psychoanalytic psychotherapy even through a modest input of weekly sessions over a relatively short period of time.

Family background, referral, and early history

Miral was the first child of an Asian couple in their early thirties who now also have a daughter Asha, two years younger than Miral. Although the parents share a common ethnic background, some of the mother's ancestors were European, which accounts for her blue eyes and white skin, in contrast to the father's dark skin and eyes. Miral has his mother's colouring, and he is the only white child among his cousins. Asha is dark like her father and the rest of the family.

The parents work long hours, and the care of the children had been handed over to the grandparents from very early on. The grandfather brought Miral to his sessions, and the grandmother would at times take one of the children to Asia for up to two months at a time. Miral went away with his grandmother when he was 2 years old, at the time of his sister's birth. When I first met the parents, Asha had been away for two months and was about to return. The couple thought that Miral had been "good" and free from his usual problems while his sister was away.

At first it was hard to get a sense of how and when Miral's difficulties had started. Gradually a more coherent picture started to take shape in my mind from the fragments of history that I gathered over time. Both the pregnancy and birth were normal, and the only comment made about this was that Miral had been small at birth. When a few months after the age of 2 years Miral returned from his holiday in Asia with his grandmother and found out that he had a baby sister, he apparently became very jealous of her. He began to adopt babyish postures and insisted that he be fed with a bottle or he would not eat. He would only sleep in his parents' bed, would not communicate, and had temper tantrums. Then, when Asha was a few months old, the children were hospitalized because they had both contracted a virus that caused them to have a high temperature and febrile convulsions. The baby recovered after a few days and went home, but Miral was kept in hospital. Apparently, during this stay a paediatrician noticed that Miral was "odd" and told Mother "not to expect much from her son", thus initiating a series of referrals that led to my contact with Miral.

It was only towards the end of my work with Miral that I was told by his mother about a traumatic event that happened shortly after his birth. When Miral was 10 days old, he began to vomit anything he ingested, and he was rushed into hospital where the doctors discovered that his bowels were twisted. He was to be operated on urgently and was transported by ambulance to another specialist hospital. In the new hospital they found that the bowels were fine and had returned to their normal position. His mother dealt with this event by cutting herself off emotionally; she ran out of the ambulance, leaving Miral in the care of his grandmother, and went wandering for hours. She told me that each time Miral had febrile convulsions, which happened several times until Miral was 5 years old, she would be reminded of that traumatic event when she thought that he would die.

Prior to my involvement, Miral had been seen by a number of specialists from different professional disciplines. He had undergone an investigation of his throat and vocal chords under general anaesthetic because of his peculiar voice; he would either talk in a squeaky and high-pitched whisper or in a very low and raucous voice. The way he spoke conveyed a sense of struggle in his throat about whether the voice should come out or not. No evidence of organic malfunction was found for this either. In the course of our work his voice had become more ordinary, but I noticed that after holidays or cancellations he would at times go back to using his "strange" whispering voice again.

He had also visited a hospital regularly for a while because of his constipation, and he had to be administered enemas on a few occasions. He would not use the lavatory to defecate, because he was scared of the toilet bowl, but would instead "leak" in his underwear and would always need to wear an absorbent pad. An organic cause for this was investigated and excluded. When he soiled his underwear he would then hide it in various places in the house, so that his parents would find it unexpectedly behind radiators or the toilet or sink. His father would get very angry with him about this.

Father gave a very painful description of how Miral ignored him, of how his son would look through him as if he were invisible, and of how he would not talk or answer his father's questions. When I saw them together, I noticed that Miral seemed to literally do away with the perception of his father. Father thought that Miral might grow out of his difficulties, given that he himself had had difficulties as a child and did not speak until he was 5 years old and had then "just caught up later" as he put it. Mother, on the other hand, was very keen to get urgent professional help for Miral. She reported that Miral would not let her out of his sight for even a moment when she was at home and would follow her everywhere. She felt exasperated by his demands and resented being forced to listen to his hour-long detailed stories.

Mother was also worried about Miral's refusal to eat. Since Miral's babyhood, eating had been a problem, and she had always needed to have the television on to distract him and put food quickly in his mouth almost without him noticing, as he became absorbed in the TV screen. For a long time, Miral would take only fluids or mashed food, and just at the time of my involvement he had started to eat more varieties of solid food, like apples and bananas. He would refuse to eat them if he saw that they had dark marks on their skin, even after the skin had been peeled off. In the course of our work, Miral started to eat increasing quantities and types of food, but in an uncompromisingly selective way. He would only accept one item of food at a time in his school packed-lunch: for a term, it was one ham sandwich; the following term, a croissant; then a jam sandwich over the next year. If his mother put in a ham sandwich or a piece of fruit or crisps during the jam-sandwich phase, they would return home in his lunch-box untouched.

At school Miral remained isolated and would occasionally bite other children. He was designated a Special Needs Child and received some support in class. He was good at maths, although his reading and writing skills were a little below average. When he became friendly with another boy in his class, he started following him everywhere like a shadow and would bite him during lunch breaks. The school felt unable to stop this from happening, and they decided that excluding Miral at lunchtimes and sending him home was their only option. The teachers felt irritated by the fact that Miral appeared to listen when he was admonished for biting, but that the very next moment he would bite again—an "in one ear, out the other" type of behaviour.

My first encounter with Miral

On first meeting Miral, I was immediately drawn to and interested in this slight boy with oversized clothes. To convey the impact that meeting Miral had on me, I shall quote from my notes of that first meeting:

> He kept looking at me in the long silence with his big dark-blue eyes, while lightly stroking a scratch on his hand and glancing at it every now and then. When I said that he had hurt his hand, that something had happened to it, he smiled, showing all of his teeth, then quickly put his index finger in his mouth and gave it a slight bite. I said that he was showing me his teeth, and he said, "One has come out, I'll be 5 soon. . . . You know, first I was a baby with no teeth, then they came out. My sister is a baby but she'll be 3 soon, she can talk now. . . . I saw a leopard when I went to Asia when I was a baby." He rolled up his trousers to show me other scratches and bruises on his legs and described

> the many ways in which he fell down and acquired them. He then said that he had seen a mouse in his kitchen but that the mouse had run away when it saw Miral. He talked in a strange high-pitched whisper that was difficult to understand. As he talked, he concentrated on pulling out tiny threads from his jumper sleeve, and when I asked what he was doing he said he was throwing away very small bits of dust. He seemed to balance himself precariously against the items of furniture in my room, and he looked unstable on his feet. I felt filled with a strong sense that he was constantly on the verge of falling down. He continued: "A leopard is bigger than a mouse, but rats they're big, they can't run away, they have nowhere to run to, no jungle. . . . Rats have only mummy and the mouse has only daddy, one each, not mummy and daddy together, one each. . . . See the tree out there, yeah? That's bigger than the mouse, and the rat, and the leopard . . . but the snake can eat the rat, and chickens, and bite the leopard, the fox can eat the mouse and chickens too. . . . If the snake doesn't eat he'll get sick. I'm sick. I sleep in mummy's bed when I'm sick. Tomorrow I'm fine and I sleep in my bed. When you do a wee you have to wash your hands before and after. . . . Mummy had long nails but they've come off, she put some glue on and now they're back again. My skin had also come off. You know when I was in mummy's tummy, yeah? In mummy's tummy I had one skin, then it came off and now I have another one."

Miral talked incessantly as his dreams and stories merged into each other. I felt very curious about the content of them, but despite my efforts I could not remember all of the details. I had a sense of being in a strange world when I was with him, and an almost physical experience of being in some sort of capsule in which time had stopped. This was a paralysing experience.

Work with the parents

Both parents had difficulties in separating from their families of origin. Mother had separated from her family when she was very young; she retained raw feelings in relation to events in her childhood and seemed to have difficulties in mourning her parents' deaths. Father, on the other hand, had a relationship with his parents that could best be described as "enmeshed".

For the first year of my work with Miral, the family lived in Father's parents' house, where the four members of Miral's family shared one bedroom despite the fact that they owned a house of their own, which was empty. Father told me that they could not move into their own house for fear that his parents would feel hurt and rejected. Being assertive and aggressive seemed to be very confused in this family's ethos. Unfortunately, it had not been possible to explore the difficulties with the couple in separating from Father's parents and establishing themselves as parents to their own children, as well as other unmourned and undigested traumatic elements in the family's background and "ghosts in the nursery" (Fraiberg, Adelson, & Shapiro, 1975). The parents conveyed a suspicion when they told me of their experience of their sessions with my colleague. They said they had felt "put under the microscope" during their sessions. I had a sense that they expected a "malignant misunderstanding" (Britton, 1998) if offered an opportunity to be understood and contained.

Britton links malignant misunderstanding to failures in containment and to difficulties in negotiating the depressive position and the oedipal situation. This formation seems to capture well this family's difficulties, both in the parental generation and emphasized in Miral's psychopathology.

Discussion of some themes in Miral's therapy

The stories

Initially Miral was not interested in playing or in the content of his therapy box of toys. His sessions were filled with streams of fragmented stories that were delivered in the form of free associations and seemed to have the purpose of keeping me very interested and firmly in my chair. At times I felt that the stories conveyed little hope that I would understand him, and at other times I thought that Miral expected me to know them all already, as if I should have been able to read his mind. Often he would mutter to himself and seemed disappointed when I could not understand him. Miral was verbally precocious, and his descriptions brought vivid and lively images to my mind. The sessions would start with him beginning with, “You know what?” Then he would wait for some sound from me that he took as an encouragement to continue talking, before he launched into a detailed story. He engendered enthusiasm in me, and I would usually try to diligently follow the complicated details in his stories. By the end of the sessions I felt lost and drained, heavy and overcrowded with fragments that I could not put together in a meaningful way. His stories alternated with endless vigorous and obsessional ball games, in which he scored more and more points, “millions and billions and trillions”, if he managed to throw the ball in particular ways and places. He would then congratulate himself on how good he was at those games. I thought that the purpose of the games was to control me, wipe me out, and to protect him from any possible impact of my comments.

I thought that the protective function of Miral’s stories and games was similar to a second-skin formation (Bick, 1968). Bick describes the gift of the gab as one of the manifestations of a second skin—a defensive structure that protects the infant or the child from the catastrophic fear of liquefying and of the contents of its body spilling out. As well as focusing attention on sensory stimuli and constant bodily movement, the baby can also resort to muscular tightening to hold itself together, so that there is no gap out of which anything can spill. Miral’s symptoms of constipation and leaking, and his shrill voice that seemed to strain through a constricted channel, seemed to be consistent with this. Miral’s extreme ways of dealing with anxiety were either to tighten his muscles or to leak in an uncontrolled way, both verbally and with his faeces.

I also thought that Miral’s use of stories could be thought about in the light of the patient described by Paul Barrows (2000), who used stories as autistic objects. Following Tustin’s ideas, Barrows made the hypothesis that such a use of stories was in aid of blocking communication: of blocking awareness of a psychological catastrophe and, ultimately, of blocking the awareness of mother’s separateness.

Through his stories, Miral was also aiming at successfully and purposefully engendering confusion in me. For instance, in an early session he looked carefully at the cow's nipples and said that it was "poo". Then he took the milkmaid woman doll and, having scrutinized her breast, he announced that it was a man footballer wearing Arsenal shorts. Two sessions later he took the cow and, indicating her breast, said that they were full of milk, and he referred to the woman doll as a woman. He smiled in recognition and seemed very pleased when I linked the two sequences and talked about his checking whether I had remembered, and whether I could tell the difference between what was real and what was not, between poo and milk, bottom and breast, and not get caught up in the confusion. While very intent at controlling me, flooding me, and not allowing me my own thoughts, I thought that Miral was also relieved at discovering that I could bear his "tricks" and retain a mind that could discriminate and remember.

The content of Miral's stories showed an intense preoccupation with teeth, a battle with his father, and some confusion about growing up, all connected with eating. He had the idea that one grows up because one eats, which in an obvious way is true. I suspect that, given his tendency to avoid eating, he might have been told at home that if he did not eat he would never grow up. He seemed to think that humans and animals were the same, and that we all lived in a chain of predators and prey in which bigger animals ate smaller ones. He must have suspected that this was how I too had become an adult. I did not find a way of talking to him about this at the time, but I had a strong sense that Miral worried that I would eat him up. Perhaps the stories also served the purpose of filling me up to prevent me from eating him. Maria Rhode describes a similar situation in relation to an anorexic patient in her paper (2000b) on the relevance of autistic anxieties in eating disorders.

Miral's stories sounded very omnipotent. In an early session he said, more or less in the same breath, "In the mornings you have to fix everything that has fallen down in the night. . . . I have two daddies and four friends and we all support Arsenal, I can't win the World Cup but Daddy can, and when I'm 7 or 6 or 5 I can win, Daddy two and Miral three. . . . I've got shoes without laces so I can't trip, but grandfather's shoes have laces, so he can trip and fall down." Miral was intent on convincing me that he was invincible, in control of his environment and even of his own life and death. He told me that he could speak five languages, that when he died he would come back to life again because he had talked to God about it, and that he could walk on water because he could swim. He impersonated wrestling champions, Power Rangers, Godzilla, or powerful Pokemons in various performances in his sessions. The performances had an almost comical effect at times, given the contrast between those powerful characters and Miral's actual small size and fragile appearance and my constant feeling that he was always about to fall. At the end of one session, he pointed to the blue veins on the back on his hands and said, "That's where the power is." He often talked about a huge dinosaur that was so big that it killed a baby dinosaur by stamping on it or by hitting it with its tail. This happened because the baby dinosaur was so small that the big dinosaur did not even see it. I thought that, for Miral, being a child and being little was felt to be intolerable, as it was linked with utter helplessness.

Miral seemed by and large to ignore my comments, or at most, after some acknowledgement of reality, he would resort to his omnipotence, as if to make sure that he continued to rely on his own self for holding himself together. I thought that, in the transference, Miral could not allow himself to feel dependent on me, since he could not afford the risk of falling and collapsing. Were he to collapse he expected there to be nobody, no mother to pick him up. I wish to illustrate this by quoting from some material from a session early in the treatment:

> He told me a story about a little leopard who had been taken away in the dark and rainy night and had to sleep on his own, but near the dinosaur and the crocodile. I said that it sounded frightening, and Miral disagreed. After a long series of adventures, the leopard returned home, because he had the power in his tail, having got this power from cutting off the crocodile's and dinosaur's tails. I commented that cutting off the big animals' tails made the little leopard feel strong. I said that this reminded me of the story he had told me of the time when he went to Asia, to the jungle, as a baby; maybe that had been scary. He looked at me directly in the eyes and said that he had

a dream; *he was on the roof of the house, then he fell off and hurt himself. Then he saw that nobody was in the house, everyone had gone; before it was only he and Mummy, but now she had left too. Then he walked and walked in the jungle for a long time and arrived at a sweet shop; they sold Arsenal things in there.*

In thinking about narcissistic aspects of the personality, Joan Symington (1985) suggests that primitive omnipotent defences that deny feelings of dependency may help the infant survive when there is no available containing object:

> I consider that this primitive fear of the state of unintegration underlies the fear of being dependent; that to experience infantile feelings of helplessness brings back echoes of that very early unheld precariousness, and this in turn motivates the patient to hold himself together. At first this is done as a desperate survival measure. Gradually these defence mechanisms become built into the character. [Symington, 1985, p. 486]

I thought that fear of falling and disintegrating, or rather unintegrating, could have been an important element in Miral's omnipotence. I also wondered whether two different states of mind should be distinguished: omnipotence with its denial of dependency as described by Symington in its survival function, and a mustering up of all available strength in the face of extreme and life-threatening circumstances, which is akin to "potency" (Alvarez, 1992).

Miral let me know about his wish to be a big, powerful footballer who was not weak and small and could not easily be flushed away. When I told Miral that he felt that it was not nice to be small, and that he felt he really ought to be big and strong, he told me that somebody's toy had fallen in the toilet bowl at school. It then flushed and the water took the toy away, "even the teacher could not save it!" He conveyed his panic at the thought of disappearing, of being flushed away, evoking in me a sense of anxiety about holding himself together that is typical of autistic studies. Later in the therapy, he showed me by his drawings the way in which a powerful tornado, a "killer twister" bringing about huge havoc and leaving only destruction in its trail, could disappear and become nothing but just a tiny pale dot on the paper.

I thought that, for Miral, anxieties about falling and disappearing had a catastrophic quality to them. At the time when his parents were considering moving into their own house with the view of getting Miral to sleep in his own bedroom, he told me about a monkey called George who was the king of the jungle. The monkey kept bumping into trees and falling into deep water. Miral did a drawing of a monkey who was walking over "a wobbly bridge", and told me that the monkey slept in a tree house and would sometimes fall off during the night. Miral added that in the new house (called "the jungle house" by the whole family because of the overgrown garden—this added to Miral's confusion) he would have to sleep in the top bunk-bed. He envisaged that he would fall off the bed while asleep at night, and he said: "If I don't move, I fall. But there's carpet on the floor so I won't hurt myself. If it's hard, it hurts." This for me highlights another feature of Miral's personality: the way in which his thinking can get very muddled. This made me wonder about an element of thought disorder.

Miral tended to make comments about things being hard or soft, hot or cold, near or far, especially in relation to my mention of coming holidays or after breaks and cancellations. The first summer holiday arrived after just over one month into our work. When I announced it, Miral told me that the ball in the box was too soft, did not bounce well, and should be much harder. He brought a hard ball from home for his next session, thereby conveying that he had to become hard and tough in order not to feel vulnerable. On another occasion before a holiday, Miral talked about the radiator in the room being cold; I thought that perhaps seeing me also as cold before an imminent separation implied some knowledge of separateness. On his return from a Christmas break, Miral kept looking at me from afar, through a paper telescope he had made.

Before another planned break from the therapy, Miral blew sheets of paper on the table with his breath, and he told me that paper was small and could be blown about and that "pieces of paper can fly away because there is no glue, the glue is still wet". I told him that he could not believe that I could have a grip on him with my mind, or that I could hold him in mind if we were not glued and stuck together. Miral's interest in glue and in sticking things together made me wonder about his employment of adhesive identification (Bick, 1968; Meltzer, Bremner, Hoxter, Weddell, & Wittenberg, 1975). On one occasion he arrived for his session with two sticker photographs of Arsenal footballers stuck to his T-shirt, one on his chest and the other on his back. He brought to my mind Francis Tustin's (1972) patient David, who felt that he built his identity by snipping off his father's bodily bits; and Maria Rhode's (2000b) thoughts about this issue of identity being a central aspect in difficulties with introjection.

Having to protect himself with something hard or spiky or even with paper around his body was a recurrent theme for Miral. A figure called "Protector" appeared in his material, drawn as a character floating in space with curved lines around his extremities and head, conjuring up in my mind the idea of crash helmets. Protecting the head was particularly important, given that usually it was the figure's spiky hair that was being shot at. It was possible for us to think together about how Miral could shoot at his own thinking and at mine. Miral also talked about an "Iron man", the character of a giant from a children's story that he liked. At the end of a session between a cancellation and a planned break, he made some paper tubes that he wrapped about his arms and legs, fixing them with sellotape, saying that those would keep him safe. I wondered about a mockery of any protective or safe-keeping function that I might have thought I had. On another occasion, Miral explained that dinosaur spikes and animals' tails and horn were there to protect them, but he would then make thrusting movements with his bottom and head, where the imaginary spikes were. He looked as if he was confusing attacking with protecting.

Dangerous feelings, murderous biting, and hatred of the father

When playing with the animals, Miral was interested in the thick-skinned and wild ones—the crocodile, rhinoceros, and dinosaur. They were protagonists of many fights in which other smaller animals would end up with their heads being eaten. He would check the big animals' teeth with his finger before they would do the biting, and once he told me that he knew they were made of hard plastic, but that their tails were soft.

> *Session 5*: He looked through the plastic bag containing the animals and said that the dinosaur had the cow's head in his mouth. (I looked as well and could not see this.) He took the crocodile and the dinosaur out of the bag and looked into the dinosaur's mouth. He said that he could see a baby in there.

I thought that Miral felt himself to be very dangerous. Before our first long holiday and his going to Asia with his mother and sister, leaving father behind, he did not open his toy box. He told me that he had seen a baby mouse in his kitchen and had taken it in his hand by its tail, and then the mouse was dead. In a mocking voice, he said that daddy was sad and cried, "Oh, where's my little mouse, it's dead". He then added that the baby mouse had died because he did not eat, because it had no teeth. I told Miral that he was telling me that he was afraid of showing me how much he wanted to bite me before the holiday, so he did not take the toys out of the box. The dead baby mouse had not eaten despite being in the kitchen where food was available; I thought that that had something to do with Miral not eating because of feeling small and not in control of the coming and going of his objects. He placated his aggression by locating himself inside his object and by denying dependency and hence aggression.

In the initial part of the therapy, Miral used to sign his drawings with "Miral and Asha Vorov". For a while his sister, Asha, was brought along to the clinic and would have to wait with the grandparent in the waiting-room while Miral had his session with me. Miral's triumph in coming with me and leaving his sister behind was apparent. Asha would often go to the lavatory in the corridor not far from my room and make sure that we heard her voice in the room. I heard from Mother that Miral would often make his sister cry by saying that he had "mummy's face and eyes", underlying their similar colour and appearance; Asha would then cry very distressed, saying that she too wanted mummy's face and eyes. Once when I arrived in the waiting-room, I noticed that the two children were playing with a baby doll. Miral was beside himself with giggles and laughter, and when he got to my room he told me that Asha had murdered the baby. He found the vicious attack on the baby very funny, and he supplied me with a detailed drawing of how Asha had used a knife and a fork and how it penetrated into the baby's body. I thought that Miral had enlisted his sister in his baby-killing "gang of two", and that her choice was either to join him or be subjected to murderous attacks herself. Towards the end of the therapy, Miral told me of a game that he and his sister had made up in which Miral was the baby and Asha was a turtle. The turtle killed the baby by hitting it with its hard shell. It was possible for us to think about Miral's idea that the only way to survive was by killing his soft infantile aspects with hard protecting and attacking turtle shells.

On his return from the first summer holiday, Miral taped all the big wild animals' mouths with sellotape, and they remained gagged for about a year. In that session, Miral was completely silent; in the course of subsequent sessions, the amount of time during which he kept his silence lessened. I thought that the gagging of the animals was a protective measure, meant to protect both of us—me from his dangerous biting and him from my retaliation. He also slowly repeated the following sequence of play over and over again, and I found myself feeling almost tortured by it: he would place the baby hippo very precariously on the edge of the couch, so that it was rather uncertain whether the baby would be left to fall or be saved. At times it fell, and at others it was saved either by the two parent animals—a hippo and rhino together—or by the mother hippo on her own. In the latter instance, she would save the baby but kick the rhino off the edge, which Miral did with relish.

I thought that Miral was showing me how angry he was with me for keeping him precariously on the edge with our sessions and for making him fall during the break. I also thought that Miral was letting me know about his dilemma of whether to acknowledge reality and the quality of his relationship with the parental couple and the oedipal situation, the "facts of life" (Money-Kyrle, 1971). Miral's preferred solution seemed to be to kick the big rhino father off, so that only Miral and his mummy remained. In the transference, I thought Miral's dilemma was whether to allow me to be a container performing both maternal and paternal functions, or to eliminate awareness of the third (Britton, 1989) and deny, for instance, the fact of holiday breaks or anything that came between us and took me away.

In one session, after mentioning his father, Miral drew a dinosaur with a horn on its head and spikes all over the body and a Pokemon with a horn on its head as well. There was a fight between the two figures, resulting in the death of the dinosaur. As this was happening, Miral drew separately on top of the page each part of the dinosaur's body as it was being destroyed—feet, tail, eyes, mouth—and he then crossed each part out as he talked about the dismembering of the dinosaur. When the demolition was completed, he drew two tiny figures at the bottom of the page, two baby dinosaurs. The one on the left had a sad mouth, because that was how he felt before the killing, and the one on the right had a happy mouth, because it portrayed the figure after the murder.

As we progressed with the therapy, Miral was able to acknowledge openly his hatred of his father, and I took this to be a pivotal moment in our work together. He told me about his mother's mobile phone, which he called his own and on which he could play a game called "Snake Two". He also told me how much he hated his father's mobile phone, because it had no games on it. A little later he told me that he wished his father would die. At the onset of our work, Miral felt that he should retain his poo and his voice and not bite his food because of the damage he felt he would do if he followed his impulses; he expected either to kill or be killed, and it was an achievement for him to be able to tell me about his hatred, bringing it in the realm of the symbolic as well as distinguishing between his wishes and reality.

Skin colours, the "Race", shortcuts, and erasing boundaries

Miral's impulse to bite might have been linked with his encountering limits and boundaries, and I thought that this was somehow mixed up with Miral's fantasies about the meaning of people's different skin colours, which is particularly relevant in terms of the different colours of his parents. Miral would often wonder about how his skin changed colour, and he would ask why when he fell and got hurt his skin became red, then blue, then black before the bruise's disappearance. While looking at the tall tree outside my window, he said that the skin of the tree was brown, and he made references to there having been lots of white snow in the garden when he was a baby. He added that the lizard was yellow, and he often identified with the lizard in his play. He said that the tree would go yellow too, then green, and then brown; it changed like Miral's skin did when he got hurt.

For several terms in the therapy, Miral used to draw circles and lines portraying cars on a racing circuit. The cars were of different colours because it was a "multicoloured race". I wondered about Miral's and Asha's race to get to me in the clinic, and about Asha's exclusion from her mother's and my "race". Miral had stated clearly that mice and rats are related but are different, and that they have one parent each, not a couple of parents. Being the only child in the family with mother's skin colour might have reinforced an integral belief in which Miral and his mother were a pair, belonging to the same hippo, mice, or rat family, so that the different one, "the rhino-father", could just be dispensed with altogether. Miral could do that through biting or by making father disappear from his perception, which imagined him away from his awareness.

Miral would often win his races by using "shortcuts". He explained to me that they were not allowed, but that one could get to the finish line faster by using them, so why not use them? I talked to Miral about his taking shortcuts in order to grow up and about him using tricks instead of having to wait to grow up in the future and one day become as big as his father, able to do things his dad could do. He replied that when he grew up, his dad would get old and grow smaller, and so Miral would be taller than his dad. When I pointed out that he was talking about a distant future and that it would take a long time before his dad grew old and small, Miral replied rather chillingly: "I know, my dad is thirty, it'll take a long time before he dies."

Miral's hatred of my boundary-keeping "paternal function" became progressively more apparent in the work and more available to be thought about, as the negative transference came more into the open. Miral would defiantly announce that he was going to take his drawings home, and he interrupted the sessions to spend considerable time in the lavatory. A first example of his wiping out boundaries came early on in the therapy when he covered the label of the therapy box with his and my name on it by painting it orange with a felt-tip pen, so that our names were not recognizable any longer. Miral also needed to blur the experience of the ending of sessions. When in our first meeting I announced that we had to stop and that I would see him the following week, he asked, "When it's my birthday, we'll have a long time, yeah?" The following time he complained that the week until the next session was too long. Later he would whistle over my words announcing the end, or would launch into a story, or would say that he was looking forward to playing with his computer game at home, which was much better than being in the session with me. Once, as soon as I said that we had to stop, he became in his mind a magic high-jumping boy and told me that he could jump up on the trees outside my window and take the little fruits, eat the berries and the apples. I looked at the tree carefully and saw indeed some little red round-shaped fruits hidden behind the leaves. I thought that if he could eliminate the limit setting, the paternal function, he would become a flying Peter Pan boy and bite it off.

Rustin's psychotic patient Holly (Rustin et al., 1997) had a hatred for pointed objects and a preference for round ones. Miral's hatred of my "point-making" function found an expression in the fact that he showed intense dislike for the points of pencils and of felt-tip pens. Once he deliberately and violently broke the point of the orange pencil that he called "carrot man"; on many other occasions he would bang the felt-tip pens against the paper very hard and in a frenzy, until their points would disappear back into the pen. Similarly, I thought that his wild riding of the couch and making farting noises over my voice as I tried to make a point were attempts at getting rid of the "paternal function" in the transference. It appeared that Miral was particularly threatened by a paternal element, which reminded him of the reality of his being a child and of his exclusion from the parental couple. It appeared that Miral experienced it as an injury and as evidence that something was being taken away from him. In a session towards the end of our work, I made an interpretation about his preference to talk to himself rather than feeling that he was with me. This happened in particular if I did not go along with what he wanted me to say but spoke my own thoughts and words. He then looked intently at my legs and said, "If there was a man here, I would put a bomb inside a burger and he would eat it and explode."

Britton (1998) described how in thin-skinned narcissistic patients (Rosenfeld, 1987), who tend to function through adhesive identification (Bick, 1968), the analyst's words are valued for their tone and not their content.

> The encompassing, embracing transference figure is regarded as positive, and the figure with penetrating understanding is the object of the negative transference. The parallel penetrating negative transference is to the third object, which is felt to be an intruder in the analysis. The affective quality of the fantasized third object, in Bion's terms, is pure K (Knowledge) divested of L (Love) and of H (Hatred). A scrutinizing object is envisaged, personifying curiosity, which seeks knowledge without sympathy, penetration without desire and possession without love. What is dreaded most is the conjunction of the encompassing transference with the penetrating transference, that is of subjectivity with objectivity. [Britton, 1998, pp. 50–51]

I thought that Miral's efforts were centred on maintaining a split in the parental couple, reflecting an oedipal situation in which there was an emphatic and totally understanding mother and a father perceived as aggressive.

About learning, confusing time, and squashing space

Miral tried to convince me that there was no difference between adults and children, and that children learnt somehow by osmosis by just being with the adult, without needing to do any work themselves. He did not take kindly to my own observations on this matter:

> He told me that Asha could drive, that she had learnt it because she was in the car with mummy as she was learning to drive. He also said that Asha had gone to the pub with friends and

> granddad. When I pointed out this wiping-out of the difference between generations, he drowned my words with mocking farting noises with his mouth. He produced strange noises with his throat too, and I thought that he was making himself vomit, but instead he burped. When I said that he wanted to burp out what he did not like about what I was saying, he started to make sheep noises. He then started counting the holes on the shelves' holders and counted up to 59. He then took little bits of the chocolate coating on his cereal bar and sprinkled them on the floor. Then he started sticking his fingers in the holes of the radiator protector. Then he put one grain of rice in the middle of his tongue and pushed his tongue in and out of his mouth many times, in the familiar lizard style. Then he broke a big piece of cereal bar and whispered, "A big rock for the Tasmanian". I remembered that in the previous session he told me about two mice, the Tasmanian Devil and Pinky, who were looking for cheese. With his finger he traced an invisible line from the tip of his shoes to the top of his head. I said it was time to stop for today, and he traced an invisible line in the air with his finger above the furniture around the room.

From the beginning of our work Miral expressed an interest in time, by drawing a sand clock and telling me how the sand ran from the top half to the bottom half, and that when time was up, it was time to move on, which also meant to start again, in a circular way. Another version of this was in a later session:

> He drew some circles: he did a big one, the usual "race" circle, and drew two smaller ones underneath the big one, which he called "cricket time" and "swimming time". He then filled the inside of the circles with orange dots and explained that those were people watching the race. He made a few big dots and told me those were gangs of football fans shouting "Arsenal". He made a shortcut line that he called "cheat", and then he covered every area with orange dots and painted orange all over it, saying that it was time. I said I remembered from the previous session that when everything became orange, it was time to move on to another activity. He then said that the big circle was "play time" and the smaller ones were "food", "drink", and

"sleeping time", and he added "practice time" and "learning time". He then started swapping the activity content of the different circles, saying that one was "swimming" and one "cricket" time. I ended up feeling very muddled and unable to follow him. Everything had been coloured in orange and was indistinguishable.

The different functions of feeding, thinking, and defecating became confused when he filled them all with orange faecal dots. I found myself thinking about Miral's controlling his object with his mouth and with his bottom in a very destructive way. I was intrigued by the image of a sand clock, something that does not retain anything as the sand flows from the top half to the bottom half. It brought to my mind associations of hollowness, and of somewhere between two and three dimensionality. Later in the therapy when Miral could communicate in a more ordinary way, he used to mention time differently, but again with the purpose of being in control of it; he told me that he wished I had a clock in the room, so that he could change the arms on the clock without me seeing it and trick me into thinking that our time was up.

I thought that as well as time, there was also a problem with space. In the last months of our work together, Miral started to spend time at the sink. Among the various things that he did there, I was interested in his fascination with wetting sheets of paper and almost becoming absorbed in looking at how the water was penetrating the paper, which led to the paper's change of colour. As we were approaching the end of one session, he put drops of water on paper with his index finger, explaining that he was taking his fingerprint. He then enlarged the dot until it became a huge circle in the middle of the sheet, making it look like a big mouth. He commented on how one could see through it. Then he made the papers stick one to the other, saying something muddled about them having to protect each other, and he made little parcels from wet sheets folded into small squares. As this was going on, I felt completely unable to follow or understand what he was doing, and I felt that I had lost him. I thought that mental space got squashed at the end of the session and that there was no room to think. I felt this strongly in the countertransference. Mental space was replaced by paper sticking together.

The "guessing" and "getting-inside" games

In the second term of our work, Miral introduced a game that remained with us throughout the therapy. After a session in which he was totally silent, he started building an enclosure with parts of the couch, and then he disappeared into it so that I could not see him. He would then make little noises with various things—a sweet wrapper, for instance—and would slowly and gradually show me bits of his finger or shoes, food, drink, or toys that he tended to have in his pockets. He would ask me to guess what it was that he had with him. A variation of this was his hiding under the desk. I would talk to him about my having to guess and not know what was going on, on my being unable to see and understand. He enjoyed my trying to guess what the mysterious objects were, and he would try to keep me going until I got it right. When he initially started this game, I had the impression that he had to take me in gradually bit by bit after the week-long absence, and that I had to have the concrete experience of remembering him, of literally putting him together in my mind. I was active in doing this and felt anxious to keep talking in the face of his silence and to keep the link going, almost as if it was a matter of life or death, the threat being that he would somehow shut down and dissolve. I thought that that was a projection into me of his terror that he would disappear from my mind. The interaction brought to my mind the image of a mother who, in an exchange with her tiny infant, puts him together by touching and naming different parts of the body, through which the baby acquires a sense of integrity of the body. As the therapy progressed, I thought that the game was assuming a ritualistic flavour, and that his requests for me to guess had the purpose of controlling me. As I started to share such thoughts with him about this, the game seemed to lose its interest for Miral, and he started to spend long portions of the sessions under the desk.

Another game that Miral developed later in the therapy was one that he called "getting inside". He would throw different coloured pens under the desk, and if they crossed a particular line on the floor it meant that they went "inside". The different colours stood for the "baddies" and the "goodies", the "winners" and the "losers". He would ask me to choose a colour, and if I did so, I would discover a bit later that my colour was the loser. Often the pens were thrown in my direction, and the target was somewhere just to the right or to the left of where I was sitting. I felt disorientated in those moments and had at times almost the physical sensation that Miral was sitting right in the middle of my forehead.

References to food in Miral's material

Miral's material was both very evocative and very fragmented, and thinking about and attempting to find a structure for it has proven quite a difficult task. Miral seemed to go in and out of psychotic moments in the sessions, and my efforts were aimed at catching him in transit between such states and then providing a describing and linking function. As Miral's mental states were subject to fluctuation, there were moments of contact and of "being with". Among the vast amount of material that he produced, he would often abruptly and unexpectedly make references to food that would take me by surprise. I would be left feeling that they were somehow important and meaningful, but that I could not have access to their importance and meaning. Miral's initial and extremely destructive orality improved, and he was able to eat more and allow himself the risk of engaging in relationships to some extent. In Miral's contradictory statements about food, the perverse aspects and the more positive ones about good and nourishing food and its function were blurred. I felt that on the whole Miral did not embrace the idea of growth and of life, but that there was a malevolence in him of the autistic aspect that made him see life as dangerous and made him opt for the perversion of choosing death. I wish to illustrate this with some session material:

> Miral drew a monster-ghost with laser eyes, sharp teeth, and four stomachs that were hanging out of the figure's body. He explained that the ghost did not need to eat for 164 days, because if he ate he would flop, his stomach would be too full, and the ghost would fall. He showed me with his body and flopped and folded himself in two. . . . He impersonated a performer, and holding an imaginary microphone he sang, watching the tree outside my window: "Water, water is for drinking, and for plants to grow. . . ." I struggled not to burst

> into laughter. After a short while he told me a muddled story in a manic way: I only understood that a singer fell into a cake and everybody in the audience laughed. He added that all the skin had come off because it was a bomb made of meat and it exploded. He then said that he hated chicken's skin."

Although this material continues to be rather hard for me to understand, I thought that Miral seemed to be a little like a ghost who admired life but did not want to participate in it. Real food implies real relationships. But Miral seemed to want to keep it as a ghost food; life and growth goes on outside the window and has nothing to do with him.

In another session when I made a comment that he did not like, he started muttering "big fat chicken, big fat chicken to eat". After a Christmas break, Miral spent a great deal of time talking about his Gameboy. He responded to a comment of mine that was aimed at trying to bring him back to the focus of the session with "When I open the fridge it stinks, the butter is all stinky, and I have to cover my nose and my mouth." He then proceeded to draw Pokemons and Gameboys. I talked to him about his avoiding his conflict with me in relation to the holiday by thinking about his Gameboys, but his mixed feelings emerged through the image of the stinky fridge. Perhaps my milk/butter became rancid because of his attacks.

In another session in the final phase of our work, after a great deal of violent material concerned with killing he talked about a helicopter spraying chocolate milk, which had a special ingredient in it that could make one strong. He also talked about strawberry-jam milk, and when the helicopter sprayed that one, trails of blood were left around. I understood that the idea was that milk could give strength but could also kill and be poisonous. Miral continued by saying that there was milk for the people inside and also for the people outside the helicopter, but the outside ones get killed. I wondered aloud about a baby who bites mummy's breast so that milk is mixed with blood, and about the inside babies getting the good stuff while the outside ones are in danger of getting killed, and how for Miral staying inside at times felt like the best option. As I talked, as if to confirm this statement he went under the desk.

Conclusion and discussion

In the course of working with Miral it became more and more apparent to me how committed he was at breaking links in order to avoid psychic pain. He would disrupt emotional contact between us whenever we touched upon emotionally painful issues. For instance, when talking about the approaching end to our work in several months' time, he would either interrupt me by asking an unrelated question, or want to go to the lavatory, or ask what the time was. Once, after a session that I had to cancel because I was not well (something that had been communicated to his parents by the receptionist), he told me that he was happy that I had been sick, because he had more time to play with his Gameboy. Miral also seemed intent at mystifying the meaning of the breaking contact and at turning the avoidance of contact into something that I was supposed to see as quite beautiful. An example of this was when he would repeatedly make a rhino and a crocodile fly towards each other in the air, making them almost crash against each other, but then flying them past each other in some sort of beautiful ballet show in slow motion.

In the material from Miral's sessions, I hope to have illustrated some connections with Bion's (1958) ideas about "attacks on linking". Miral's attacks on linking could be seen in this light as threefold: he attacked his own capacity for thinking, he disrupted the link between his and my mind, and he managed to seriously disrupt the links that I was able to make in my own mind. For Bion (1962), the patient envies the couple engaged in a creative act from which he feels excluded. He has a painful emotional experience that can amount to hatred. "This hatred contributes to the murderous attacks on that which links the pair, on the pair itself and on the object generated by the pair" (Bion, 1962, p. 100). Similarly to what Williams (1997) described in relation to her patient "Martin", Miral's attacks on linking were at the core of his mental violence and possibly a source of his emotional deprivation. This contributed to making my focus on providing a link-making object and a relationship in which both maternal and paternal aspects of containment are included, a very difficult task—and at times something that I felt was almost a hopeless one. In spite of this, Miral did grow bigger and became more ordinary and a little better able to interact with others in his everyday life. I perceived him as less shallow, more solid, and less two-dimensional in the sense described by Meltzer (Meltzer et al., 1975). At the time of ending our work together, however, I experienced a resurgence of anxiety about Miral's mental state, as he seemed to spend an increasing amount of time withdrawing from reality again in a sort of "psychic retreat" (Steiner, 1993). He found it very difficult to negotiate the loss of our work, and he tried to persuade me that it did not matter at all.

The family as a "system" also seemed to have changed in some ways as a result of Miral's involvement with the clinic, even though they had not had regular sessions. One year into the therapy, the family members moved into their own house; the grandparents have, however, remained very involved with looking after the children, as Mother had started to work some nightshifts. In the meeting when Mother told me about the traumatic incident in Miral's babyhood, she also talked about deprivation in her own childhood, and she was able to think about getting some individual psychotherapy herself.

Miral remains in many ways a child using a "no-entry" system of defences (Williams, 1997). In the course of our work, I heard of a figure called "the guard". Apparently, this is an electric toy complete with a laser ray that gets activated and sends an alarm when somebody approaches. This "guard" seems to keep the entrance into Miral's room at home clear of intruders. Miral does play in his room, but he would not sleep in there. The toy stays there to make sure that nobody goes into Miral's room when he is not there. This inimical guard seems to be a mockery of a paternal door-keeping function, as it is completely under Miral's control.

As became confirmed by Miral's history towards the end of the therapy, it seems that he had experienced massive failure of containment (Bion, 1962) when his life was threatened in infancy. His mother could not help him at the time; a relationship between the two of them developed in which mother seemed to be able only either to run away from what she felt were Miral's and Asha's ganging up against her, or to passively give in to her children's demands.

In conclusion, I shall try to reflect on what might have occurred in Miral's internal world that had contributed to his being the child I have come to know. My main hypothesis would be that Miral's psychopathology was in part due to an early malfunctioning of the skin as internal container, in the light of Bick's seminal paper of 1968. Such impairment had led to confusions about internal spaces in the self and in the body, and to difficulties in taking in food, in learning, and in engaging in relationships. The establishment of a good internal object was impaired. As for the origin of this disturbance, I speculate that both Miral's fantasy attacks on his objects, as well as inadequacies in the actual caregivers in terms of their capacity to contain emotional experience, have combined in an unfortunate way. My experience of Miral was of a child with damaged internal objects and with a leaky container full of holes in its skin, one that could retain very little at times, as expressed in his symptoms. Miral had great difficulty with separation and with allowing himself to feel dependent in his therapy. For Miral, being separate seemed to be confused with being excluded. Perhaps this could be traced back to a primary deprivation, a deprivation at the breast, and to a resulting sense of emptiness while at the same time feeling that mother and father were endlessly enjoying all that the child feels he does not have access to. In this situation of deprivation and need and greed for the object, it becomes impossible for Miral to remain outside and allow his objects their freedom. Instead of bearing the imagined mystery of what happens between the parents in the concrete parental bedroom and in fantasy, Miral feels drawn to entering inside his object. His actual and continuing sharing of his parents' bed does not help with this. Once inside, he feels persecuted and haunted by damaged and bitten objects, and thus a vicious circle is perpetuated.

CHAPTER FOUR

A latency boy's eating difficulties and their meaning in his inner world

Stephen Briggs

> "George said he did not like food very much. I asked him what he did eat. He said 'pasta, bread, and chunks of cheese.'"

Eating a diet of pasta, bread, and cheese in sufficient quanti ties is not, in itself, life threatening. It is, however, extremely restricting. This was the diet of a young boy, George, whose treatment I shall describe in this chapter. A further restriction was that each food item had to be eaten separately. Cheese could not be eaten with bread, nor with pasta. Sandwiches were definitely not on the menu. He refused vegetables, meat, and fruit. He did begin to eat sweet things fairly soon after his treatment began, but his diet consisted totally of dried or desiccated foods. Though George, who was 8 years old when treatment began, kept himself alive with his diet, it pointed to emotional difficulties. The food he ate, the way he ate it, and the food he did not eat all held important meaning about his inner world. The aim in this chapter is to explore the meaning that was attached to George's eating patterns as they emerged in the course of his therapy. I shall concentrate initially on how a picture of George's inner world emerged over the first year and a half of his therapy. I shall then discuss the process of working through the difficulties that occurred during the rest of his therapy, which lasted for four years.

Background and framework

When George's parents, originally from overseas and now living in London, asked for him to be seen at the Tavistock, they were concerned not only about his diet, but the way this seemed to be linked with tension in the home and the difficulties they experienced in organizing family life around these eating habits, to the point that George was seen as quite exasperating. Particularly, they described difficulties that would arise if George were to be away from them. He could not, for example, go on school trips, because he could not eat when away. At school, the parents were worried that he was not learning, and that he lacked concentration. The school also expressed concern, especially about his inability to write and the fact that he was often in trouble, with a reputation for bullying other boys.

George had a sister ten years older than he was. She had failed her university examinations, and this was one of a number of stresses in the home in addition to George's problems. George's father, a professional man, had had to cope with a reduced income in recent years. His mother had begun to work as a personnel officer when George was 7 years old. Of George's early experiences, parents said that George had breast-fed successfully but had accepted only lump-free dehydrated food after weaning. He had, nevertheless, been an easy baby and toddler, and difficulties seemed first to emerge when he was unhappy in attending playgroup, aged 3. George was seen on three occasions by a female colleague, who found that he was verbal and cooperative when talking about subjects of his choice. When it came to thinking about the problems that his parents were concerned about, he seemed to disengage, or switch off. The assessment concluded that he might be able to develop his interests in a creative way, but that he appeared to have significant difficulties in his development. The feeding difficulties were part of an overall picture, in which there was evidence of difficulties in learning, in relating to others, and in separating.

The recommendation was that George would be seen for therapy on a once- or twice-a-week basis. Initially, I was able to offer him a once-weekly time, with the thought that it could be increased later to twice if this was thought beneficial. Additionally, I would meet with the parents at the end of each term to review progress, and they would meet from time to time with a colleague. Both parents were in agreement with this plan and understood that I thought that George's eating and behavioural difficulties were part of an overall problem. Both parents were, in fact, anxious about George, and somewhat at a loss themselves, but they also conveyed a quite sceptical feeling about the plan for therapy.

First three months of treatment

During the first three months of treatment, George presented, in the material of his sessions with me, consistent evidence of his developmental difficulties. As had happened with his assessment, George did not express to me any view of his own difficulties. Instead, he spoke very much from his own perspective. His conversation was lateral, free-floating even, and made very little reference to external reality. I was left in my mind with "hard" facts and thoughts about his difficulties, which he showed no signs of either wishing or being able to discuss directly with me. I began to formulate the thought that he was preoccupied with two states of mind: one was strident, violent, and explosive; the other, soft and tender and created an atmosphere of wistful longing. There appeared to be a sudden and extreme change when George moved between these two states of mind. For example, in the third session:

> He told me he will make a paper aeroplane, set fire to it, and throw it. His voice became strident and his eyes lit up. He abruptly looked down and was quiet. He looked up at the picture on the wall and began to hum a tune, and then his mouth made sucking movements. His head was turned away from me and he seemed engrossed. Then, drifting back he

caught sight of me in the corner of his eye and stopped his sucking movements.

When he was quietly sucking, I felt that I was seeing an infant who was quite fragile, and this made me feel that I should be cautious with him, and try to protect this vulnerable side of him. This was in direct contrast with the strident, violent boy who appeared to become excited at the thought of his destructiveness, and who suggested to me that a more vigorous kind of containment was required from me.

The wistfulness, which evoked an absent maternal figure, was apparent when he spoke of relationships to remote objects, such as stars, whose light "takes ten years to reach here, that is since before I was born". He also appeared to be preoccupied with the loss of the female therapist who had assessed him. While he had spoken eloquently in his assessment of his interest in plants, this subject was conspicuous by its absence in sessions with me. He told me there was nothing growing in his allotment—except leeks, which was the only vegetable in this waste land. George's perception of what might grow with me in his therapy seemed to suggest a feeling of desolation, possibly linked with loss.

Instead of talking about plants, he spoke about animals. He discussed an array of animals, some of which were exotic, and which often had a dangerous or phallic quality, or both. In the first session, his suspicion of being trapped by me, and his intention to avoid this fate, was suggested by his admiration of crabs: "Some crabs are really clever," he said, "they let go of the bait as it comes out of the water." This suggested that, for his survival, there was an either/or choice, in which not eating, not taking the bait, was the smart thing to do. He immediately imported this concept into the relationship with me, for as I started to speak, to interpret, he interrupted me with a different subject of his own. The pets that he said he would like to have included a slow-worm, a tarantula, and a scorpion, and he maintained that they were only dangerous if their young were threatened. He seemed to suggest that should my interpretations sting or bite, then he would like to be in a position to retaliate. The image provided by George's talk about these animals suggested a deadly rivalry, but hinted at a sense of vulnerability also. He seemed to be telling me that it was going to be difficult to take anything in, because, in his perception, he was being invited to incorporate something quite dangerous. He needed to summon reinforcements in his vulnerability, in the form of his counter-attacking pets. He gave a further illustration in the second session:

> He asked me if I had been to the Devil's Cauldron. It is a whirlpool that has been carved out of the rock, and the water is pure. He paused and then added that he had put a paper boat on the water. It filled with water and sank. He stopped talking and looked around the room, at all the walls and the floor. I said that perhaps he felt himself to be the boat in the pure water, and perhaps he feared I might be dangerous to him, his boat, and that this room could be like the Devil's Cauldron. He smiled at me and nodded.

His smile was ambiguous; though he accepted the interpretation, I was left unsure how this had affected him, as though the interpretation sank like the boat. He gave no sign of being relieved by it, and he seemed to feel that what I said was confirmation of his reason to fear the words I used, and what I saw. He later talked about two teachers, one called "good eyes" who could see what was happening, and the other called "bad eyes" who missed everything. George was adamant that he preferred "bad eyes". At times I felt he would prefer me to miss what he was showing me, though by his own definition, I would have become "bad".

This confusion of good and bad seemed to be described in his story about the Devil's Cauldron, as the place where the water was pure, or good, but also as a dangerous or bad place, unsupportive of dependency, where he was unprotected from the storms of the outside world. Similarly, the fact that the water was pure implied that there was, elsewhere, another sphere where there was contamination.

George provided abundant material that suggested both the dangerousness of the world in which father was a central figure and the contamination of the food within it. The combination of dangerousness and contamination left him with no belief in adult benevolence. In his assessment he had spoken of small plants that were undernourished because two tall trees took their water away.

With me, he communicated a feeling that adults were stupid. He told me of a frog, in the pond in his garden, that tried to mate with a goldfish—"stupid thing", he added, contemptuously. This appeared to stand for a belief that the link between mother and father was bizarre or grotesque and was the linking (or mis-linking) of two quite different species. He may have developed this idea to obliterate paranoid or envious feelings that the adults (tall trees) were depriving rather than sustaining him.

Dangerousness, contamination, and mis-linking were evidenced in his relationship with me, in these first sessions. He appeared to experience me concretely, as paternal, and at a part-object level. He had already mentioned to me his wish for a slow-worm as a pet and that he would keep this in his pocket. In the ninth session, he played with two marbles, a paper-clip, and a "bulldog clip". The play was both sexually graphic and ambiguous, causing me to think that he may have had some sexual experience, which may have been abusive. The material also suggested that he was expressing a particular state of mind:

> He took two magnetic marbles from his pocket and rubbed them in his hand. He took a paper-clip and allowed it to be attracted to the two balls. He tried to lift the balls with the clip, and they fell into his hand. He inserted the paper-clip between the balls. He looked at me, checking, then produced a bulldog clip from his pocket and put the paper-clip into the "mouth" of the bulldog clip. He pushed the clip in and out, gripping it strongly with the bulldog clip/"mouth" so that the paper-clip became elongated.

I felt at the time that I would have to keep an open mind as to whether he was illustrating an actual event, but I decided to interpret the material within the transference. I pointed out that all the items he was playing with were his—that is to say, that he had brought them to the session—with the exception of the paper-clip. He then played again with the clip and the balls:

> I said I wondered what was happening now. He said, "not sure". I said the bulldog clip seemed to be a mouth. He said that was what he thought too. I asked "and the balls?" and he

> replied "gobstoppers". I said the mouth had some hard things to chew—a metal clip and the hard balls. He said, "cannonballs".

This seemed to present a very difficult issue to think about, and even more difficult to discuss. There was some evidence that he was wishing to crush my potency, in terms of the sexual symbolism with the balls and the paper-clip, and that he did not like me understanding this. At the same time, my responses to him were very cautious—as I also found it difficult to name what may be involved here. Certainly it felt impossible to talk about the sexual imagery directly, and yet this may have also prematurely restricted the range of meanings that could be seen in this sequence. I thus felt myself attempting to stay between two extremes—namely, passivity (or being impotent) and overfeeding (or being "elongated" or potent).

One aspect of this was that he was suspicious and fearful of me, and that he thus had some hostility towards me which he wished to remain covert. Throughout, he was alert to a danger and ready to scuttle away like the crab, to withdraw. If possible, he would surreptitiously rob me of my potency.

George's phantasies appeared to be concerned with both a significant split inside himself and a difficulty of bringing father and mother together in his mind. When they did come together, he had a terrifying, persecutory experience, which threatened his survival. He demonstrated that when he had to make a transition from the "pure water" of mother to the "hard" world of father, he was left bare (as he described my room) or empty, through his refusal to be trapped into taking the "bait", and paranoid about connecting facts to ideas. Food and intellectual integration had become persecutory for him. In this way, food became contaminated in a gruesome way.

He graphically described contamination of food when he told me about mushrooms. He knew the names for those that were poisonous, and those that were edible. He himself did not eat them:

> "They [his parents] thought they could eat them [the mushrooms] but they got stomach-aches. You can tell if they are poisonous because they go blue if you dry them. Some mush-

> rooms are very edible," but he did not eat them because they might have woodlice in them. They had dried some other mushrooms and then cut them in slices to see if they were edible. They were very edible.

This seemed to be quite a graphic representation of his eating difficulties. Mushrooms had to be dried and dissected, and they concealed either poison or live parasites. The notion of live animals in the food turned dangerous and grotesque when George described his friend's "chop suey":

> He looked at me and told me "his friend has a hobby. He is mad. He collects dead wasp-stings as well. He has over a hundred of them and he makes a chop suey with them. He carries them in a pencil-case and takes them to school."

I thought George's friend represented a part of himself, and the description of this unsavoury mixture, which could be placed inside a container (the pencil-case), took me further in understanding his reluctance to eat food in which there was either a sense of life (as in vegetables or meat) or a mixture (as in sandwiches). The notion of dissection of meat, being linked with an attacking paternal function, came to the fore when he told me about some pheasants his father had:

> George said they would be getting covered in pheasants' feathers. He sounded quite shrill and angry. His father had two pheasants in the car and he (George) will dissect them. He wants to see their hearts and lungs. His mother had got some gizzards, but she had cooked them before he had been able to dissect them.

The strident tone returned in this communication. The attack on the object through dissection, his morbid curiosity about insides, and his paranoia that gizzards, like mushrooms, should be carefully dissected to ensure detection of poison and parasites, all left me commenting rather lamely on the rather peculiar nature of his curiosity:

> "Well, you are interested in the inside of things", I said. George replied, yes he was; he always had been, but he did not know why. He always wants to see how things work.

And he continued eloquently, ensuring that I did not address his "not knowing why".

George's aggression towards small animals (babies?) and the pheasants (or mother's body?), when linked with his descriptions of himself at school, illustrated some of the difficulties he had in this area. He told me about his interest in origami, and how he used this "gentle art" to make water bombs. He would throw them at his fellow pupils. He made a bomb in a session and demonstrated its use:

> "You get this paper and bang it on the desk." He demonstrated with his arm, swooping down, looking at the table as though he would hit it, but his arm simply came down through the air. He said you can only do it once and then it breaks.

This explosiveness was linked with a theme of intrusive penetration. He thought that a large Christmas tree would burst through the ceiling into the room above. The notion that this "banger" could only "bang" once before it broke suggested a bee or scorpion sting, revealing a destructive fear George held: that his own explosive anger would destroy him, through ripping his skin apart.

These first sessions with George helped to formulate a hypothesis that there had been some form of catastrophe at weaning, in which he had left the pure water of the breast-feeding relationship with mother for a persecutory world, epitomised by father's degraded and dangerous genitals. He appeared to have identified with this intrusive object, and, in his resistance to making emotional contact with me, and his fears of tearing himself apart, he seemed to show a fear that he, himself, might be broken into. His identification with the dangerous object was seen when he sympathized with a shark, who was a "much maligned creature". Yet a shark had teeth that were instantly replaced, and it was therefore always defended, and not prone to a self-destructive explosion. He knew, he told me, from discussions he had with his mother, that he too had a "mouthful of teeth" that grew all together at the time of weaning.

Persecutory and paranoid phantasies, together with his mistrust of me in the transference, created a difficult situation in his therapy. Though he was able to tell me, through his stories and images, a great deal about his inner world, he restricted severely how much could be taken in from me. Like the crab, he maintained a number of defences against experiencing a "live" relationship. If material was not previously dissected, so to speak, it could be dangerous or poisonous. If it was dissected and dried, it lacked nourishment. This was George's "Catch 22". In the moment-by-moment exchanges in the sessions, I began to see that George's control of me and of my words was central to his difficulties. His aim was to prevent any live contact between us. If there was live contact, he immediately attacked it. On the other hand, if my interpretations did reach him, they had the effect of taking him over to the extent that he experienced the situation I was talking about quite concretely. Thus, in the second session, George's acceptance of my interpretation about the Devil's Cauldron was followed by a loss of grip on the relationship, and on himself:

> He pushed himself into the corner of the couch, holding the arm of the couch with his hand, and then he seemed to lose his grip, becoming floppy, almost muscle-less, and he appeared to be drifting off to sleep.

He then spoke about a hollow object, a bauble on a Christmas tree, that might easily fall and break. The suggestion was that his skin was either brittle or fragile, through its inner emptiness. Given his very restricted eating pattern, he could well have experienced this emptiness in a physical way. The idea that he was like a bauble that could smash to pieces if touched also suggested a phantasy or fear of violent disintegration. In that he was wary of the soft or brittle skin being broached or damaged, he attempted to make a tough skin for himself, which would be always defended, like the shark. Yet, he could not totally cover up or rid himself of his sense of something tender being lost to him. In the reference to the bauble, he was also expressing a relationship between a fragile part of himself, the bauble, and the Christmas tree, which he had already mentioned as possessing violently intrusive qualities. The mechanism that brought about separation was not mentioned, and he seemed to simply have a fear that he would be severed incomprehensibly from his object.

If the qualities that made a beneficial link between objects seemed beyond his comprehension, he contributed with his hatred to this lack of understanding. When opportunity arose in the sessions to talk about his problems at school, he told me he "hates comprehension". Though he knew a lot about esoteric subjects, such as the names of mushrooms and plants, these were related to his own idiosyncratic researches. When it came to understanding, or writing, he found himself unable to cope. When discussing his learning, he oscillated between two states of mind. First, he adopted a superior omnipotence, knowing better than adults, who were "stupid", like the frog and the goldfish; second, he was persecuted by his helplessness and smallness. He gave me a view of the despair he felt at achieving tasks at school in comparison with grown-ups, particularly his mother:

> He said he was behind in history. He had to write 40 words. But that is nothing. His mother did some exams and she had to write 10,000 words a week . He would never, never, never do that.

This statement confirmed the overwhelming nature of development. Persecuted by a sense of his own smallness, looking ahead with despair, turning away with hatred from growth, he felt he would *never* do what grown-ups do.

As George approached the first therapy break, his wistfulness and nostalgic sense of lost union loomed large. He seemed sad to leave mother in the waiting-room, as the sessions had begun to stand for the place where hated growth took place. He also began to explore, in his tangential and elliptical way, what a separation from his therapy would mean. He spoke of a remote contact with a star:

> He asked me where I lived, and was it in the same place as he lived? If I lived there I would have seen the red star in the sky. It takes ten years for the light to reach here—that is, from before he was born. He looked away from me, preoccupied.

He had not been able to keep up the defensive, tough "take it or leave it" approach to his therapy that he admired in crabs. At the beginning of his therapy, he wished for a thick skin so that he could refuse the bait. But attentiveness to his states of mind had revealed his rather intense dependency. Thus the focus of anxiety and danger shifted from contact with me in his therapy to the cessation of contact at the end of sessions. He appeared to experience this as a sudden breaking of connection, rather like the bauble falling from the Christmas tree, and he protected himself by taking control. He took to asking me the time, so that the end of sessions would not take him by surprise. He told me he had seen the Bayeux tapestry, which was a marvel because it was seamless. Again, he gave evidence that his preferred relationship was one of fusion, but he was able to think about separation and its meaning for him. He asked me if I thought a tie could keep him warm, which pointed to a slim hope of being nurtured in his relationship with me by the tie between us. Is it possible, he seemed to be asking, that this therapy could offer him warmth and protection?

Development over the rest of the first year of therapy

When he returned to therapy after the break, he indicated to me that the holidays had left him with an empty or dead state of mind. The first session had a deadening quality, with George usually prefacing his responses to me with a "no" when I tried to engage him. He then told me about a moth he had placed in a safe:

> He said he has a safe in his room, a portable one, and there was a dead moth in it. I asked him to confirm—did he say he had a dead moth in the safe? He said yes, it was not dead when he put it there. Anyway he had taken the moth out. He added that that left just air in the safe and after saying this he blew out his cheeks and exhaled.

This was a striking image of his experience over the break, in which what he had taken to be a safe place became a deadly incarceration. Once the dead moth(er) is taken out, there is emptiness. When he blew out his cheeks, he confirmed a link between himself and the safe. He had seemed to say to me that just as I had left him without contact with me over the break, he had in an imitation of me left the moth to die. He then spoke about his idea of cruel paternal care:

> "George does grow bigger," he said, "but he has warts which he does not like." He said they were not that bad, they did not hurt. His dad had bigger ones and he pulled them off with a pair of pincers. No trouble.

In this state of mind, attachments are simply cut off or torn away. He appears to feel that he is a hated object, a wart that I pulled out with a pair of pincers in the holiday. He continued with the theme of tough rejection of feelings of loss:

> George said I should have seen his budgie. It lay on the floor of its cage and by 8 p.m. it was dead—kaput. He said his dad would give him a tenner. I queried, a tenner? and George said that was what it cost to buy another budgie.

This materialist way of coping with painful emotions was necessary when painful feelings could not be held on to for more than a moment. To survive he needed to be ruthless, and he took the cuckoo as his role model:

> He said he had a cuckoo clock in his room—had he told me before?—and then he made some paper animals (origami) that had wide mouths. I said these animals and the cuckoo represent someone who throws babies out of the nest. "Yes," he said, "the cuckoo keeps the nest all for himself. The cuckoo knows what he is doing", he added, deliberately.

His certainty that the cuckoo was under an imperative motivation driven by a fight for survival needed to be taken seriously (Symington, 1985). George's object relations were too tenuous to drop this particular defence, or belief, that survival depended upon occupation of the nest and the summary eviction of the soft, easily disturbed baby part of himself. Thoughts of separation appeared whenever he made contact with an object, so that his grip on the object was lost. He told me that a friend (again, I think, representing himself) was only just saved by a member of the ship's crew when he fell from HMS *Belfast*. At least in this example there is an idea of a watchful person, the crew member, who notices and acts in a helpful way. He felt he needed to attach himself more securely to the therapy, and he enacted this in a literal way by tying himself to the couch.

In his play with paper (origami), he made many aeroplanes, and he was particularly preoccupied with the way they landed, trying to ensure a smooth rather than a bumpy landing. He made a mountaineer and talked of climbing down from a campsite to a beach, which I interpreted as his wish to reach me, while keeping a grip, rather than falling.

George's willingness to make emotional contact with me over the issue of separating and falling was linked with his willingness to tell me how helpless he felt with the task facing him:

> He came to the table and took some paper, saying he was making a crane (he emphasized it was a bird, not a machine). He folded the paper and said he would like to make hundreds of them. He had heard of a girl who had made 10,000 origami cranes, and she had done this to try and save her friend's life, as the friend was ill. She did not make them in time and the friend died (he said this with some contempt). "Well, it is not possible to make so many", he added.

In origami, a crane is a particularly important symbol of completeness. Here, and repeatedly afterwards, it became the subject through which George attempted to make reparation. He was easily discouraged by the size of his task—and the idea that failure could have lethal consequences. The sense of failure to repair the damage affected both of us. He communicated to me that I had taken on a task, in treating him, that was going to be beyond me. At times I too had a feeling that matched this communication. The image of the girl who tried to make so many cranes had a sense of urgency—that there was a time when it might be too late. He seemed to be urging me to speed up and not be so slow with his treatment. In turn this seemed to be a projection of his own awareness of his slowness in development.

George then began to eat more and to change his patterns of behaviour at school. He told me he might win a prize for the most improved pupil in school. His parents informed me that he had no longer problems with bullying, and that he had started to eat some salads and a wider range of cheese. George became, however, preoccupied with cheating. He made an origami cube out of paper and said that if he used sellotape he would be cheating. In this way he began to reassert his attack on the help I provided. The purity of one substance, or fusion, or seamlessness was not to be easily given up. If growth meant accepting a link with another, then he repudiated growth. He communicated with me that I had tricked him into development, and he resumed an anxious and suspicious relationship to me. Everywhere there was an outbreak of growth, and it led to contamination:

> "Moths are everywhere now," he said, "they laid eggs in the muesli, and rice. I found a maggot in the rice—but at least it was corked.'"

He became anxious about the quality of support that was offered by the couch:

> He put his hand under the couch. He felt round the underside and then stood up and lifted the cushion. He said that this was "weird, badly weird". I said "weird?" and he said he had expected to find a triangle, not a square (pointing to the frame). This was not very strong he said, it was weak. I talked with him about the changes he had told me about—his eating, school, and that he seemed unsure whether I could give him a strong enough place at the moment, whether I could support him firmly enough. He said that at least *Crystal Maze* was still on. He asked me how long there was left in the session. and I said twenty minutes. He said it was like *Crystal Maze*. "There, they say the door is shut and there are two minutes to go."

Although the evidence suggested that maintaining emotional contact with me, and beginning to tolerate anxieties stirred up by experiences of separation, was helping him develop in his capacities to relate and to learn, he was convinced that something awful had been perpetrated on him. He became intent on attacking growth and support. For example, he played with his shoes:

> He looked at his shoes and took them off. He said they were too small, and turning them over he said they have no grip. He looked inside the shoes and pulled out the insoles, folding them and saying that he did not need them any more. He said they were worn out and asked me if he could throw them in the bin. He put his knees in the shoes and shuffled round the room, saying he was a midget. I said that it occurred to me he was growing bigger and he was quite worried about it. Perhaps if this continued, particularly if he started to eat different things, he would feel that I would say he would not need to come here any more. I said that this was not the case and that we could meet together as long as we both felt he needed to come. He looked at me quite warmly, even lovingly for a few moments.

The attempts I made to help him with his anxieties at this point were not sufficient to offset his attacks on me and his own development, and he reverted to his previously restricted feeding regime.

Therapy from twelve to eighteen months

For George, the summer break was an interminable experience. He returned to his therapy wishing to be hard-skinned and tough, as "hard as a conker":

> He asked me how he could make his conker really hard. He had tried salt and vinegar. He does not want his conker to be broken. His only worry was that he would have to remove the skin to make a grip on another conker.

He is toughened up by being left, and I am perceived as being "hard" in that I dismiss him from my mind and my room. There are now two options, neither of which is free of anxiety: to become really hard, and risk being violently shattered by contact with another, or to painfully peel the skin away in order to make contact. The anticipation of making contact is feared and potentially hurtful. He appeared to expect me to be ready to skin him. Images of the dissected pheasants returned to my mind.

Something is new in this material: an awareness of pain, which is projected into an anticipation that I would treat him quite cruelly—by skinning him. He tried to keep his awareness of pain at bay, through concentrating on the need for survival—the suspicions and persecutions of the paranoid–schizoid position. The depressive position was deadly, a place where he would sink without trace, like the boat in the Devil's Cauldron. It seemed that when he sensed the approach of a depressive moment, he immediately turned away or attacked it.

He began to communicate an unease about his own "oddness", and his fears of madness. In one of his origami games, George spoke about "laying a square egg". His preoccupation with eggs, maggots, larvae, and the cuckoo made it clear that the "egg" referred to himself, or, more accurately, to one of mother's babies who happened to be him. He was an "odd egg", a square (p)egg in a round hole, so to speak. He was the "baby" who was in therapy, and who experienced the session as a "Crystal Maze". He was capable of moments of emotional contact, but I was also confronted with an aspect of George that resembled Richard III, who said in his despair:

> ". . . since I cannot prove a lover
> To entertain these fair well-spoken days
> I am determined to be a villain."
>
> [Act 1, Scene 1, 28–30]

George, in a similar vein, decided to make a virtue out of necessity and attack all of mother's babies. He turned to his older sister as a model of rebellion, and he enlisted his father as a co-conspirator; he identified with the shark in *Jaws* and attacked the container itself. He needed to establish where I was placed in this constellation—was I a potential gang member, or was I beyond corruption? He began to express his suspicion openly, and, in so doing, the issue of bugs, maggots, and larvae were gathered into the transference and were invested with traces of symbolism:

> George looked me in the eye and said that at school they have a bug detector. I said, a bug detector? He said it was like the police used to find where there were bugs. There was one they found in one room and it was like a ladybird. I thought of addressing his suspicions of me, but he had moved on, shuffling a pack of cards he had brought with him. He said he needs a piece of paper to help the cards grip the table. He added that he wanted to make a house of cards. He stood some cards on end, and they fell down. He glanced up at the ceiling and said he would build a large house, twenty floors high. He said they would all fall down, except the bottom layer. I said, the bottom layer was strong enough to withstand the top layers falling down? He nodded, and the four layers he had built fell down, the bottom layer remaining standing. He said, "Like that."

I commented on the difference between the bottom layer's stability (his successful breast-feeding experience?) and the rest of the layers. I spoke also about his anxiety of falling, being dropped, and his suspicion that I might not be genuinely able to help. Since his therapy took place on one of the upper floors of a building with five floors, it was inescapable that he was thus destroying this room. He began to talk about food:

> He said they have a blues band at school—they call it a greens band. He and his two friends are called "vegetable blues sing the greens". He said, "it is funny isn't it? It's greens instead of blues." One friend sings "I've lost my brussel sprout and I want to shout", and the other says "I've lost my carrot and I'm so down". He laughed. I asked what he sang. He would not tell me. He said it was just his friends. They were really crazy. Really crazy, just mad. I asked if he was eating vegetables at the moment, and he said he was not, in a tone that suggested that it was a silly question. I said we both knew this was something that was important to him and we were here to think together about his eating difficulties. He nodded and looked me in the eye quite warmly.

He seemed to appreciate the directness of this comment of mine, and his post–summer-break hard shell fell away for a moment.

Perhaps it was important at this point not to interpret his destructiveness, as it may have been received as a cruel communication which may have further inflamed his attacks on me and himself, though I also felt that he had somehow found a way, in his manic vegetable band song, to keep me away from talking directly about his violent and fearful thoughts about his therapy.

In the next session, he was more in touch with the process of separation and left some space for me to make interpretations about these feelings and preoccupations:

> He rummaged in his pocket and pulled out what seemed to be an enormous number of objects—screws, hooks, strings, pipe-cleaners, and, as the objects stuck together, there was clearly a magnet too. He looked at me and then made a space on the couch next to himself, tied three wheel-shaped magnets to a piece of string, and repeatedly picked up and dropped a number of items. I watched quietly as he played for some time. He then swung the magnet over the floor and bumped it several times along the floor, and the items—hooks, screws, and so on—fell off. He picked them up, lifted the magnet high, and then let the magnet and objects fall into his hand.
>
> I said that this seems to be about the breaks between our sessions, but in using the magnet he is showing me that he is in control. He said, immediately, not grudgingly, "I suppose so." He carried on playing, bumping the magnet on the floor so the objects fell off, and again picking them up. I said these changes always seemed to be beyond his control. Either I went away or his parents arranged holidays or school put cricket on the same day as his session here. He nodded and continued playing.

His play with the magnet continued. He illustrated sticking to the table as a means of avoiding separation, and separating with a bump when he thought about leaving. The magnet fell apart as he tensely imagined the sense of falling apart for which only the toughest skin (a hard conker) could be enough to prevent disintegration. Each time in this sequence I was able to interpret, and he was able to follow my interpretations without a withdrawal.

Discussion: the meaning of the feeding difficulties

George began his therapy with a restricted and restricting diet. In his relationship with me, he showed that the diet had a specific meaning and illustrated the problems in his inner world. First, the refusal of vegetables and meat, and indeed anything live, resulted from his fear and hatred of lively contact with others. His preference was for dried and desiccated food, and for exerting control over its intake. He had quite paranoid fears of taking in something that was contaminated or poisoned, like mushrooms or moth eggs, and he seemed to have a fear of something bursting into grotesque life within him. These paranoid fears seemed connected with his emotional experiences of being in contact with someone else, especially in a dependent relationship. This made him feel small, and the task of development was felt to be overwhelming and he hated it for having this impact on him.

Second, he took his food singly, taking care not to mix the elements of his restricted diet of bread, pasta, and parmesan cheese, though these three foods formed, generally, usually two pairs (pasta and parmesan, bread and cheese). He told me he hated sandwiches. George had an idea of the maternal which was idealized and tender; in contrast, his relationship to the paternal was based on an idea of a cruel, cutting, and harsh father-figure. He aimed to keep the two—maternal and paternal—apart. If they got together, they starved him of sustenance—the two tall trees—or they produced a grotesque couple—the frog and the goldfish.

There emerged in the course of George's therapy a further contrast between the pure, fused, or seamless ideal relationship with mother and the "contaminated" world of growth and development, which included separateness, experiences of separation, dependency, and the need of others. The pure relationship was a single entity (one), which he repeatedly referred to—in references to the pure water of the Devil's Cauldron, the Bayeux tapestry, the cube of paper, which should hold together without sellotape, and distant stars. These references were often accompanied by wistfulness or nostalgia, and they held a strong feeling of a wish to fuse, to be *one*. In contrast, to be aware of *twos* or links, between people and things, meant an inevitable awareness of the possibility of separation. When, in his therapy, George could tolerate the idea of separation, he could achieve moments of contact with me and an increasing capacity to explore the meaning of separation, in which I was permitted space to interpret, and he gave the impression that he was able to take in these interpretations. Often, however, thoughts of separation were accompanied by images—such as the bauble on the Christmas tree, and the conker—in which there were quite terrifying thoughts of falling apart and breaking, or having skin torn off in an excruciating way. *Twos*, couples, or links between couples seemed synonymous with some terrifying and awful feelings and thoughts. Additionally, these experiences introduced thoughts of a more malignant nature, including intense hatred and attacks on others and on the vulnerable part of himself.

George communicated to me that he wished to be hard and impervious to the excruciating emotions that were involved in being in emotional contact. In truth, he was not able to achieve this hardness, for the tender, vulnerable part of himself was too alive and too troubling to him. The restricted diet was a manifestation of a defensive organization, which permitted some relief from these anxieties—through avoiding them—at the cost of suspending growth and development (O'Shaughnessy, 1981; Steiner, 1993).

George often wished to be impervious to feelings, and to develop a hard, tough, or thick skin to overcome the emotional impact on him of his vulnerability. Although he aimed to develop a "no-entry" system of defences (Williams, 1997) to restrict what he had to take in, and to some extent succeeded in this, especially with regard to his food intake and his learning, he was far too "porous" to be described as impervious. He was easily flooded by his own experiences of vulnerability and others' comments. He was thus primarily "thin-skinned", which Britton (1998) defines: "In the thin-skinned mode the self seeks to avoid the objectivity of the third object and to cling to subjectivity" (p. 46).

A picture therefore emerged of the infant George who had an idea of a good relationship, and some experience of it, but, in that he was easily overwhelmed by what he was required to take in, he seemed to have experienced being projected into rather than being contained (Williams, 1997). For George, weaning appears to have been a catastrophe, where the loss of the breast-feeding relationship he had been able to develop (although the suggestions are that he was very passive in this relationship), combined with the sudden growth of a mouthful of teeth, left him extremely persecuted, hating development, and in a depressed relationship to the lost relationship with mother. This relationship then became idealized as a union, or fusion, so that he also lost a relationship with a good internal mother. It can then be hypothesized that his depressed feelings after weaning were not contained, and that the misunderstanding, or misfit , between George and his parents gave him an experience not just of containment being absent, but of an active projection into him, or "convex" containment (Briggs, 1997).

This configuration left George in a precarious state, facing severe internal difficulties. His more paranoid and persecuted feelings and his resort to esoteric modes of learning cut him off from the "real" world of others and indicated fairly intense psychotic anxieties, which were persistently disturbing his inner world and his relationships with others. His hatred and explosiveness, which appeared in his material as violent phantasies, usually directed at tender or infantile aspects of himself and others, indicated a particularly intense inner conflict that was potentially self-destructive. I have discussed how, in the process of experiencing some containment in his therapy, he relaxed his very rigid grip on his eating patterns, this inner conflict intensified, and his persecutory anxieties increased. These underlying conflicts—the absence of any good figures in his internal world, and an intense battle between vulnerable "thin-skinned" and sadistic "thick-skinned" aspects of himself—were kept in check by the defence of his restricted eating pattern. In his therapy, these needed to be known and contained. I shall briefly illustrate the working-through of these conflicts.

Development in the course of George's therapy

As George became less passive, and his rigid grip on his defensive organization relaxed, he was confronted with fears of madness and with suicidal ideas. He began to face with me the problems of aiming to obliterate the parents rather than take in from them. Magagna (2000) has pointed out that "The risk of suicide is always present when the anorectic child, freed from some defensive strategies during the assessment or in the course of treatment, attempts to face such emotions as sadness, desperation or a sense of severe persecutory guilt or depression" (p. 55). Through the third year of therapy, George made an increasing number of references to suicidal ideas. In the fourth year of his therapy, ideas of suicide and madness were linked with experiences of separation. He discussed with me a forthcoming weekend away from home at a scout camp:

> "They have gas canisters and if you throw them on the fire they really explode. Someone, a woman, wanted to commit suicide and put a gas canister on the fire. Then she changed her mind and ran out of the house. The house exploded." I asked him if he recalled talking to me about suicide the last time he went to scout camp. He said no—did he? I said he did. He had told me about a suicidal friend who had a chain-saw. He said, oh yes he did. He remembered this, it was a friend who is quite mad. I said it seems he puts some very explosive feelings of his own into going to scout camp. He is talking to me about something that feels very dangerous to himself and other people. He looked at me quite steadily, perhaps taking in what I said.
>
> He said, well, he'll be sharing a tent with two boys who are quite mad. They have six-inch knives and they are really quite mad. He paused and added, well, he has a six-inch knife himself. I said that he is aware now that these feelings belong to him.
>
> He said that another friend is not going to the camp. He is a nerd. I asked what he meant by "nerd". He said, well, you should just see his jumper. It has pictures of lambs and flowers on it. He sounded most contemptuous. I said that he is making fun, quite cruelly, of the very vulnerable George, who really does find it difficult to have ordinary worries about being on his own. Instead he has to make himself as hard as nails. As hard as what, he asked? I repeated, as hard as nails. "As hard as rock", he said, correcting me. "Yes," I replied, "this is the way you feel you have to be."

Thus George was able to have a rather direct discussion with me about these very difficult feelings and thoughts. He remained engaged with me in the session and accepted my interpretation that he was projecting his vulnerable feelings onto the other boys.

Moreover, he had the effect of filling me with worry about his absence on this trip. This seemed to indicate that he was able to use me as an object he could put his feelings into, and that I could keep them in my mind rather than prematurely returning them to him.

The approach of puberty added further turbulence and upheaval. There were more direct discussions about his eating. He began to eat more, and he told me about this:

> He said he didn't like sandwiches much. He hates them. I said he hates them. He said, well, except for peanut butter or marmite sandwich or syrup sandwich. But not cheese. Well, he doesn't mind if "it's French bread and—not Gruyère [he was struggling to find the word]—Emmenthal. That's ok. But ordinary bread and cheese. Ugh, I hate that."

The problem of sandwiches was here addressed at a literal level. The "sandwich" of his conflict between the vulnerable, depressed, and sadistic, violent parts of himself, which he aimed to control and keep apart, was also engaged with. In particular, he was more able to be open with me about his depression. Alvarez (2000) has emphasized the importance of depression that results from a child's feeling of not having the resources to make reparation, and who "may feel incapable of meeting the demands of a needy or damaged object that is felt to be beyond their strength to repair. The blanket of despair seems much more total and all parts of the self and the object seem to be engulfed in it" (p. 40).

George's feeling in the Devil's Cauldron, his inability to face writing words, and the overwhelming task of making 10,000 origami cranes all are examples of this incapability and the consequent engulfment. In the later part of his therapy, George was able to discuss depression from a position of being separate from his object. For example:

> He said "Shoes". I said, shoes? He said, "Your shoes, they look like they are light on the outside and dark in the middle, and a bit weird." He was quiet and clearly wanting to say something, but not able to. He undid his laces and then did them up again. I said it seems there might be something more he might like to say about this. He nodded. I said, well perhaps it's something to

> do with whose shoes he wants to be in, as in the phrase, "I would like to be in your shoes." He said, "I wouldn't like to be in your shoes." He was quiet again and seemed very heavy. He looked at his shoes and then at mine. I said, it is some time since he had been like this with me, seemingly unable to carry on thinking. He said that he was tired and had tons of homework. He then talked about wishing to hibernate. I said that hibernating seemed to him the solution when he was faced with heavy feelings. I said that, in fact, he was showing me he gets depressed. He said "Yes." I continued to talk about this, and he listened. He looked down at his shoes and rubbed them. He said they needed a polish.

The discussion of depressed feelings proceeded with difficulty, but it was closely linked with greater engagement with me and with the world around him. This included doing homework, and aiming, therefore, to work towards adulthood rather than appropriating a false and fraudulent adult status through omnipotent phantasies.

Conclusion

In this discussion of George's therapy, I have emphasized the meaning of the particular eating patterns that George presented at the beginning of his therapy. The meaning of his diet has been shown to constitute a defensive organization, in order to avoid the intense anxieties that arose in him whenever maternal and paternal aspects came together. When he relaxed the rigid control of this regime, a highly combustible internal conflict came to the forefront of the work in his therapy. In the course of the work with him, the crucial aspects of this conflict were discussed. It was essential to this work to enable a capacity in George to have greater contact with others, to have a firmer grip on his objects, and to be able then to discuss these violent and depressed parts of himself. Thus some movement towards accepting growth and development took place.

CHAPTER FIVE

Aspects of the body image and sense of identity in a boy with autism: implications for eating disorders

Maria Rhode

My aim in this chapter is to describe various aspects of the body image of a boy with autism as they emerged during his therapy between the ages of 6 and 9 years, and to explore connections with his picture of his primary object and with fears concerning eating and being eaten. I shall attempt to relate patterns in this child's material to similar ones in adult patients with eating disorders.

It is a common observation that anorexic patients often have a body image that can be unrealistic to the point of being delusional. Someone who is emaciated to a life-threatening degree can still think of herself as fat and can perceive professionals' attempts to save her life by getting her to eat as evidence of a hostile determination to make her ugly and unattractive. Anorexics seem to be preoccupied with the space their body occupies even more than with how much they weigh (which may indeed be experienced in terms of fitting into the space below a particular line on the scales). Space that is occupied may not feel like the person's own legitimate space, and it is often unclear into whom any food that is eaten will go. For example, an anorexic patient described by Henri Rey (1994) felt that she contained both a mother and a baby in a mutually destructive relationship, and that she had to starve "herself" in order to kill the mother and free the baby. Sheila MacLeod (1981), in a book written after her recovery from anorexia, emphasized that pregnancy was the one time when she experienced none of her usual panic on approaching the weight of 8 stone. It is as though the fact of physically containing a baby gave her permission to expand. Joyce McDougall's patient Georgette, who had suffered from anorexia as well as from a variety of psychosomatic ailments, was preoccupied with issues concerning skin as a body boundary—both her own and her mother's (McDougall, 1989). Georgette experienced herself as sharing completely in the analyst's life, to the point of talking about "our husband". In the course of treatment, her inability to eat shellfish was resolved when she associated its smell to that of the parental genitalia. Such accounts call to mind the commonly reported confusion seen in anorexics between eating and sexual maturity, between food and babies. However, they also highlight fundamental issues of identity, in terms of whose space is occupied by whom.

Children with autism are, like anorexic patients, preoccupied with issues concerning their identity and survival; again like anorexic patients, they may attempt to cope by exerting complete, delusional control over their environment. When this is not possible, their sense of helplessness and panic can be overwhelming. Frances Tustin (1981, 1986) has discussed material of anorexic patients who she felt showed pronounced autistic features. More recently, Barrows (1999) has noted the importance of such features in a young woman with bulimia.

From Tustin (1972) and Meltzer et al. (1975) onwards, autistic children's body image has been described as bizarre, unstable, two-dimensional, subject to a binary split (Haag, 1985; Tustin, 1981). In this chapter, I wish to consider a number of vignettes to illustrate different ways in which Anthony, a boy with moderate to severe autism, experienced his body. Although he did make considerable progress during treatment, that will not be my focus here, nor shall I attempt to describe how his body image evolved over time. His sense of identity appeared to be very unstable, often varying according to the physical space within which he found himself, and thematic links emerged very gradually. Inevitably, such a thematic presentation must provide a picture of Anthony's therapy that does not do justice to the repetitions, the sense of confusion, and the difficulty of forming any clear impression of who was doing what to whom. Part of this difficulty was a function of the obscurity of the material and of my own shortcomings; part, I believe, was a function of the instability of Anthony's sense of identity, some aspects of which feature in the material I shall discuss. Though some of the patterns that emerged appear to me suggestive, much must remain speculative, as must the links I shall later propose with material from patients with eating disorders.

Between the parents

At the time of his referral at the age of 6 years, Anthony's teachers described him as highly intelligent but extremely withdrawn. He took virtually no notice of other people; when he spoke, it was in a repertoire of voices not his own, and his speech did not appear to be communicative. If his parents took their eyes off him for a moment, he would damage the house and threaten his younger sister with a knife. In a family session, he sat wedged between his parents, smiling in a way that they described as happy, but which appeared to my colleague and to me to be strongly tinged with cruelty. Although Anthony's parents were loving and concerned, and realized that he needed help with his destructive behaviour, it appeared to be difficult for them to recognize and respond to some of his emotions.

Birth and bodily mutilation

Cruelty of more than one kind was an important theme from the beginning of Anthony's treatment. He enacted over and over again what looked like the catastrophic birth experience that Tustin described in "Psychological Birth and Psychological Catastrophe" (1981): falling head first off the desk into the void, he would struggle to reach the safety of a chair. As he fell, he clutched the drawstring at the waist of his tracksuit bottoms as though it were an umbilical cord that was supposed to stop him from falling. He twisted his mouth into a tortured, distorted shape. It was as though the broken mouth, which Tustin (1972) has described as being the autistic child's essential experience of bodily separateness, were the immediate concomitant of his tortured "birth" from the desk and the associated loss of the umbilical cord that had joined him to the mother-figure.

In turn, Anthony inflicted tortures on the doll family, twisting their heads and limbs until they came off. The dolls' house would be balanced precariously on the edge of various pieces of furniture, only to be lifted high in the air, to the accompaniment of menacing growls, and spun around and hurtled groundwards until all the furniture fell out. Anthony muttered, "Dorothy"—presumably an allusion to the film, *The Wizard of Oz,* in which Dorothy's house is lifted into the air by a tornado. I understood this both as Anthony's way of conveying the chaos of his experience of bodily separateness, and also as the representation of his attacks against supposed inhabitants of a mother-house, on whom he was visiting his sufferings just as he had on the doll family.

It was difficult at this point to judge how far these attacks went beyond a communication of his own experiences—whether his cruelty remained a matter of his being in projective identification with a cruel internal figure, or whether he had come to enjoy it for its own sake. What was certain was that Anthony did not expect to be able to communicate his experiences to another person without having a catastrophic effect on them. For example, early on he cut deep, cruel gashes into the sides of a plastic beaker; months later, he filled it with water and described the leaks as "Lady crying". Such a leaky, crying internal object provided him with no support. When he placed the beaker in the dolls' house, he showed me repeatedly how easily the house tipped off the edge of a chair. It was as though his own tornado-like experience of birth had been cruelly transmitted to an object—the plastic beaker—that had been damaged in the process, and the whole sequence had been internalized and thus perpetuated. It is interesting that Anthony was, in fact, hypersensitive to the sound of other children crying. This was often the trigger for his attacks on them—probably, it seemed to me, as much with the aim of trying to reassure himself that his actions were not responsible for the crying as with the aim of getting it to stop.

The cruelty of the impervious combined object

Tustin (1981) proposed that physical birth could be experienced as a psychological catastrophe if the mother were unable to provide emotional containment of the infant's experience in the form of what she called a "mental uterus". Anthony seemed to experience being on the outside of anything or anybody as meaning that his body was under threat and that no one noticed or understood this. He often banged violently with his knees into the metal radiator, producing a loud clang. His knees could not, of course, penetrate the metal. Instead, they were forced wide apart, as though his legs might be broken off at the hip-joint. Such fears of being dismembered or "disjointed" are frequently met with in children with autism (Haag, 1985, 1991).

Similarly, the shut door on the dolls' house seemed to be pushing Anthony into space. He would ring the doorbell, pleading, "Pleeease help me", with a falling intonation as though he were dropping off the edge, but without eliciting any response from inside the house.

Anthony appeared to blame the mutual absorption of a twin-like parental couple for this imperviousness to his experience of falling and of being mutilated. Balancing a cow on its muzzle on the surface of a mirror, he pointed at the reflection and said, "Mummy and Daddy". He spent much time on the telephone, speaking in his mother's voice to someone he addressed as "Darling" while ignoring me completely: he vividly conveyed how totally this conversation between the parental couple obliterated anyone who was not part of it. At other times, Anthony smiled, enraptured, at the telephone receiver, which he held as though it were either a mirror or a microphone. He looked as though he were a star in love with his public and basking in their adulation; or a narcissistic mother receiving the admiration of an adoring husband. Indeed, I was informed that he came into his own on any occasion that involved performing.

It seemed, then, that Anthony experienced the parents—who in reality were devoted to him and concerned for his welfare—as uniting against him to form a cruel and impervious combined object. Before a holiday break that came sooner than expected because of unavoidable external factors, he impassively and methodically cut body parts off the toy animals—muzzles, tails, ears, paws, or hooves. The animals all pleaded, "Please don't do this to me", but the process of mutilation continued as though no one had heard them. After talking to him about this at length, I eventually stopped him—not to do so would have felt like colluding with the ethos of the concentration camps.

Anthony appeared to attribute different aspects of this experience of mutilation to the maternal and paternal elements of a cruel parental couple. The active cutting off of body parts seemed to be the function of the father, represented by such figures as the evil Darth Vader in the *Star Wars* trilogy who cuts off his son Luke Skywalker's hand; or by the Giant in *Jack and the Beanstalk* who threatens Jack with being killed and devoured, and whose menacing growls Anthony often adopted. The mother-figure, on the other hand, seemed to express her cruelty primarily by ignoring the victims' pleas. Anthony's mother, who battled courageously to cope as cheerfully as she could with circumstances that were often overwhelming, did in fact occasionally say "Yes" in a way that might sound as though she were humouring someone. He once produced a startlingly accurate imitation of this tone of voice and then commented, "Cruel mummy". It appeared that the cruelty that featured so prominently was both to do with Anthony's experience of bodily mutilation and with what he felt was the wilful ignoring of this experience by an impervious mother-figure completely taken up with a "darling" husband who was her own mirror-image.

Like Tustin's patients John, David, and Peter (Tustin, 1972, 1981, 1990), Anthony was preoccupied with getting hold of a powerful "extra bit" that he seemed to think adults possessed, and which made them immune to terrors such as his. Possession of this "bit"—he sometimes felt this was my watch, ring, or scarf, which he would try to grab—would presumably make things all right. This was a magical solution, and it was ultimately unhelpful as it inevitably left him feeling that he had no proper foundation and that his object was either damaged (the leaky beaker) or vengeful (the giant-father).

The tripartite object: the nature of the link between the parents

Shortly after a holiday some two years into treatment, Anthony began to insert his hand down the crack between the seat and back cushions of an armchair while muttering about a one-pound coin. It took me some weeks to realize that he was referring to a current advertisement for McDonald's. This showed a burger bun, opened up to look like an armchair, with two burgers as cushions, one lining the back of the chair, the other the seat. The pound coin—advertised as being all that was needed to buy this Double Burger—was shown poking out between the two burger "cushions". Anthony behaved as though he felt it to be a powerful, magical object, like my ring or scarf, which would procure the possession of twice as much burger as normal. At the same time, the structure of the Double Burger called to mind the "Mummy-and-Daddy" bull-and-cow reflected in the mirror, who seemed hinged by their muzzles like the back and seat of the chair.

I wish to emphasize several aspects of this tripartite model. One is the similarity to the position, wedged between his parents, that Anthony took up at our first meeting, as though he were a pound coin both linking and separating them. Second, if the pound coin conferred ownership of the Double Burger, this implies that Anthony saw himself as being in a position to possess both parents orally, at the same time as preventing them from feeding each other (Klein, 1957). Later in treatment, when Anthony's phantasy objects were separating out from each other and becoming more ordinary as well as easier to tell apart, he would make the calf feed in turn from the cow's udder ("Yummy milk") and from the bull's genitals—early phantasies that are familiar from the work of Melanie Klein (1932). This shows a considerable development from the previous position in which he tried to grab my watch, ring, or scarf as part of a life-or-death struggle, rather than feed from organs acknowledged as being part of someone else. As I have already suggested, this earlier stance resembled that of Tustin's patients David (Tustin, 1972), who tried to build up his identity by snipping powerful bits off his father, and John (Tustin, 1994), who was surprised to find that "the red button *grows* on the breast" (p. 7) rather than being part of his own mouth. In children with autism, a constellation in which two people are engaged in a life-and-death rivalry for a single essential thing can often be the form in which a three-body relationship is manifest. On a part-object level, this would mean that the nipple is not experienced as a vital link between mouth and breast or bottle: instead, mouth and breast are felt to be competing for ownership of it.

The tri-partite structure of "The Face"

When Anthony was himself between the parents, both joining them and separating them, it was as though he had become this link that they were supposed to fight over. The cruelty of his smile at such times was the only clue to the emotional complexities involved. The fact that his parents generally found it was only possible to get Anthony off to sleep by lying down next to him may have fed into his idea that he had the power to interfere in an oral intercourse between them (as McDougall, 1989, suggests) by forming a couple with whichever parent was available.

When Anthony was not between the parents, the experience of waiting appeared to take on the terrifying qualities of being physically mutilated and ignored, which I have already described. It then seemed that the parental couple that was united in excluding him was linked by something between them that was not himself. The following vignette illustrates some of the properties of this "something". Instead of being an emotional link between the parents, it appeared to be a physical join (the glue that he used to stick a cloth "plaster" to the wall). At the same time, it dislodged Anthony from his preferred position between the parents, as though it were a rival child. Finally, when at the end of the play sequence Anthony ate the glue, this seemed an example of the confusion between food and babies, and it illustrates how feeding can be less a matter of taking in nourishment than of separating and damaging an impervious mother–baby–father threesome.

> When I came to the waiting-room to fetch him, Anthony responded by jumping at me suddenly, growling in the Giant's menacing voice. Once we arrived in the therapy-room, he quoted from a story about Thomas the Tank Engine, who disobeyed the Fat Controller (both characters in a series of well-known children's stories and television programmes). Thomas fell down a mine from where he had to be rescued. Anthony seemed to feel that taking over a father-figure's powerful voice in order to break through a boundary (the interval between sessions) meant literally falling into an abyss inside the mother or the therapy-room.
>
> He then noticed three indentations in the wall, arranged as though they were two eyes with a mouth below them. He traced around them with his finger to make the outline of a face, saying, "Poor eye, poor eye" ("poor 'I'"). He made a sticking-plaster for the eye from a strip of J-Cloth and stuck it to the wall with glue from a solid glue-stick to cover the indentation. One end of the strip curved away from the wall like a label. Anthony tugged at it, as though testing whether he could pull it off; then he tugged at the tongue of his shoe, and with his teeth at bits of loose skin on his fingers. Next, he pushed the stick of glue upwards so that it protruded from its case, and he pinched off little bits to eat. When I removed the J-Cloth "plaster" from the wall in preparation for the end of the session, Anthony rolled the glue remaining on the wall into little balls resembling nasal mucus, and ate them. He then picked bits of mucus out of his nose and ate these as well.

Anthony seemed to think that the holes in a face—the eyes and mouth—were signs of the damage that is caused when the child bangs into a "brick-wall" object (the "cruel mummy") that is taking no notice of him. He appeared to equate them with the mine down which Thomas the Tank Engine had fallen when he disobeyed the Fat Controller. It was as though the wait between sessions had been imposed by the prohibition of a controlling father-figure. Anthony's sudden aggressive jump in my direction, presumably in defiance of this prohibition, served the purpose of making me take notice of him—in his terms, it made eyes in the Face. (Indeed, both at home and at school, Anthony had got into the habit of getting himself noticed by being naughty.) However, being noticed seemed to go hand-in-hand with damaging me as a mother-figure, so that he "fell down the mine" into me and needed rescuing. "Mending" the damage in the wall by restoring its tripartite structure (using glue to stick the J-Cloth skin over the hole-eyes) makes the eyes blind again: the child seems to face the dilemma of choosing between a blind object and a broken one. Eating the mucus-like glue seemed to be a matter of ingesting the substance that should have bound together two essential parts of the Face. One could imagine a nursing baby looking into its mother's face and blaming its own feeding for any sadness or withdrawal to be discerned there (Meltzer et al., 1975). Later in treatment, Anthony did in fact manage a better solution: instead of sticking the J-Cloth over the eye "holes", he turned them into seeing eyes that no longer looked broken, by adding a coloured pupil with a felt-tipped pen.

It is interesting to note similarities with material from a patient with encapsulated autistic features described by S. Klein (1980). This woman spoke of her feelings of insecurity in terms of a structure of bricks collapsing: "it became apparent that this was due to her attacking the cement which bound her together, namely [the analyst's] interpretations. Her own association of cement with semen showed her hostility to the creativity of both parents, who were not allowed to come together in her mind" (p. 396) This same patient had "a dream in which *she had two swellings on either side of her body* to which she associated sitting between two pregnant women at a dinner party"; this was linked with "omnipotent appropriation . . . of her mother's genital and breast creativity" (p. 396). Some of the basic patterns in Anthony's material (attacks on glue or cement; being between two people) appear very similar to this. However, his picture of the parents is at this stage far less differentiated. In the adult woman's material, paternal and maternal creativity are represented in different trains of thought, and sitting between two people leads to taking over the qualities of the parent of the same sex, rather than to forming a threesome with a couple that is physically joined together.

The body image and the image of the object

The integrity of Anthony's own skin seemed to depend on the integrity of his object's skin: he plucked at his cuticles and tugged at the tongue of his shoe in just the same way as he tugged at the protruding J-Cloth "skin" of the Face. Similarly, he appeared to equate his own balls of nasal mucus with the balls of glue, whether these were pinched off the glue-stick or extracted from the Face after the J-Cloth-plaster-skin had been peeled off.

The pun of "poor eye" and "poor I" highlights this equation of self and object. Two different processes seem to be involved here. Firstly, there is the process that Bick (1968, 1986) and Meltzer (1974) have called "adhesive identification" and that Tustin (1994) has termed "adhesive equation" with the aim of emphasizing the complete identity between self and object and the lack of any acknowledged space between them. This equation takes place on the basis of surface qualities, so that in the absence of the object the child collapses. The second process is that which Winnicott (1967) has called mirroring: he proposes that the baby derives its fundamental sense of existence and goodness from what it sees reflected in its mother's face. I shall return to these issues later.

Cannibalizing babies: devouring and being devoured

Anthony's dilemma, *vis-à-vis* the Face, of having to choose between a blind object and a broken one, was a fair representation of the drawbacks involved in his strategy of getting attention by attacking his siblings or children at school. It was as though he blamed them for whatever distress he experienced: if he were not between the parents forming a threesome with them, then the other children must be. While he could generally count on getting attention by attacking another child, the quality of this attention was, of course, hostile. It is as though attacking the baby that was felt to be joining the parental couple and forming a tripartite structure that excluded him damaged the link between the parental couple, who then came together to attack him. In Bion's terms, "links . . . being impregnated now with cruelty, link objects together cruelly" (Bion, 1957, p. 50). The confusion between food and the link between the couple (the balls of glue that Anthony ate) implies a model in which eating damages the couple by extracting the link between them, which appears to be experienced as a very primitive version of a *baby* that participates in the parents' relationship. Eating and growing becomes confused with separating a parental couple that belongs together (Rhode, 2000). By implication, the child who has done this makes himself vulnerable to being devoured by the parents when they come back together, as though they formed a giant, vengeful mouth cruelly snapping shut.

Indeed, Anthony enacted chilling scenes of mutual cannibalism between the generations. Baby lambs cannibalized adult sheep ("sheep bleeding", as he said) and were in turn cannibalized by the adults. This felt like an eternal, unbreakable vicious circle. Nothing was resolved: the protagonists merely exchanged roles. Anthony would appear as aggressor or victim depending on which physical space he occupied. In the therapy-room, he growled in the voice of the devouring Giant; in the stairwell, he pleaded not to be devoured.

"Eating the grass": horse, grass, and shadow

As a counterpoint to these sequences, Anthony presented what seemed at first to be a more benign alternative. Tipping the horse, cow, or bull forward so that it was balanced on its muzzle on the table, he would say, "Eating the grass". This looked like quite a realistic representation of a cow or a horse cropping grass in a field, and it felt like a welcome contrast to the gruesome scenes of cannibalism between the generations.

However, it struck me that the position of the grazing animals was the same as that of the cow that Anthony had balanced on its muzzle on the mirror, forming the mirror-image that he had described as "Mummy and Daddy". I then noticed that he seemed to be looking fixedly "into" the table, rather than at its surface or at the horse, cow, or bull balanced on it. Following his glance, I saw the shadow that the animal cast on the table, and which was usually so faint that I might well have overlooked it except for Anthony's fixed concentration.

What had appeared to be a representation of a herbivore harmlessly grazing therefore took on a more problematic quality. If one thinks of the grass—the "in between" element in this tripartite structure of animal, grass, and shadow—as occupying a position analogous to that of the glue-link in the Face's tripartite structure of wall–glue–J-Cloth, then the implication follows that the horse is nourishing itself by eating the grass at the expense of its own shadow, which becomes a starved, damaged, and potentially vengeful object.

This suggests a mutual antagonism between two objects that are not identical—whether between a mother and father who are not mirror images of each other, between the generations, or between different aspects of Anthony's personality. Taken on that level, the material calls to mind Bion's imaginary twin (Bion, 1950), or the identification in Ancient Egyptian ritual of one twin with life and light, and the other with the underworld and darkness (Rhode, 1994). Barrows (1999), whose bulimic patient with significant autistic features described herself as a shadow person, linked this with an identification with her parents' dead siblings whom they had been unable to mourn. Anthony's parents, in fact, suffered major bereavements, although I do not know enough details to be able to suggest a meaningful link.

Discussion

Anthony's anticipation of trouble from the horse's shadow is an example of the seeming impossibility of achieving what Bion (1962) called a commensal relationship, in which two objects share a third to the benefit of all three. Instead, his world was one in which life-or-death struggles for powerful bodily "bits" (Tustin) led to an eternal see-saw, in which there seemed no alternative to being either a completely helpless victim or a cruel and implacable victimizer.

In this world, the experience of links was highly aberrant. The nipple did not seem to be a vital link between Anthony and the breast or bottle, but something to be fought over, like the grass between horse and shadow. Similarly, the link between the parental couple was experienced as the cruel cause for the mother-figure's imperviousness to his distress. This area has been explored by Britton (1998), who proposed that a baby with a mother-figure who is incapable of performing alpha-function may continue to cling to her for the sake of survival while blaming the third party of the oedipal triangle for the blocking of nonverbal communication. For such a baby, the closure of the oedipal triangle—the recognition of the link between the parents—is experienced as a disaster. To this formulation I would add that another child, as well as a father-figure, may be blamed for the blocking of nonverbal communication; I would also add that this area of experience presents scope for confusions between a mother-figure's mental imperviousness or *pre*-occupation, and her physical *occupation* by a rival (Rhode, 1999; Wittenberg, 1975). These confusions seem to me to be in large part responsible for the aberrant way in which children with autism experience their own bodies.

This leads me on to the way in which Anthony equated his own skin with the skin of the Face. As I have suggested, two processes seem to be involved: adhesive identification (Bick, 1968, 1986; Meltzer, 1974) or adhesive equation (Tustin, 1994); and mirroring (Winnicott, 1967), in which the baby sees himself reflected in his mother's gaze. Although a fuller discussion goes beyond the scope of the present chapter, I would suggest that the instances of adhesive equation in the Face material, in which Anthony seemed to experience his skin as being *identical to* the Face's skin rather than *like* it, may be to do with his feeling that the Face was blind to his individuality. This problem would be compounded by the seeming impossibility of getting himself noticed—of creating seeing eyes—without damage to the object. This links with the importance for the child's development of being seen as himself (as he must be if the mother's vital capacity for alpha-function is not to be interfered with) rather than as the representative of figures from the parents' internal world. This line of enquiry was opened up in Fraiberg's seminal paper (Fraiberg et al., 1975) and has particular relevance to autistic spectrum disorder (Barrows, 1999; Earnshaw, 1994; Klauber, 1999; Reid, 1999; Tischler, 1979; Tustin, 1994). It would make sense that a child who does not feel mirrored in a way that validates his own individual identity should fall back on adhesive mechanisms leading to a sense of being identical to his object.

Freud described equations between self and object as occurring in unresolved mourning (Freud, 1917) and in certain perversions (Freud, 1919). Rey (1988) observed a similar lack of differentiation in psychotic patients whose search for a cure turned out to be the search for someone who could cure their damaged objects. In Anthony's case, adhesive equation with an object that he perceived as damaged led to the perpetuation of his anxieties concerning his bodily integrity. It also made it possible for him to exert delusional, magical control over his object by means of manoeuvres with his own body, since this was felt to be identical to his object's body. For example, when he was frightened of falling down a crack between desk and chair, he might try to deal with this by clamping his lips tight together—as though making sure that no crack opened up between his own lips would ensure that no crack down which he might fall could open up between desk and chair.

On a few occasions when Anthony did feel recognized, he enacted a benign feeding experience in stark contrast to the scenarios I have described. Equally, he sometimes genuinely felt that there were enough resources for three people. (This was expressed in terms of the nursery rhyme, "Baa, Baa, Black Sheep", in which there are "three bags full: one for the master, one for the dame, and one for the little boy who lives down the lane".) When this happened, his cruelty in the therapy-room diminished, and he did not appear to feel in danger of being devoured in the stairwell. Otherwise, he seemed to cope with the dilemma of devouring or being devoured by not maintaining a stable identity of his own. Instead, his identity shifted rapidly through the three aspects of the horse–grass–shadow. None of these positions was satisfactory or even safe. The horse (the dominant, cruel part of Anthony's personality, which allowed no scope to his softer side, and was primarily expressed in the therapy-room) was constantly on guard against the shadow. The shadow (I saw this as Anthony's softer side, which he seemed to feel threatened by and which suddenly overtook him in the stairwell) seemed to be allowed no proper existence of its own. The grass—the "in between" element—got eaten: even being between the parents, since this was done with the aim of separating them, left Anthony vulnerable to being obliterated by two parts of a vengeful "mouth" snapping shut.

Indeed, any configuration that resembled the two parts of a mouth appeared to be highly dangerous. When Anthony was falling off the desk, he seemed to feel safer, however unrealistically, if he could hold on to the stretched-out drawstring of his tracksuit bottoms. However, when he doubled the string back on itself, it immediately became threatening: he slid his hand between the two strands, and they appeared to "bite" it off at the wrist. A sense of safety, however delusional, seemed to flow only from the undifferentiated continuity of an umbilical-cord-like string (Winnicott, 1960), or from a tripartite structure in which the baby was felt to be the link between the parents and to participate in their relationship.

In time, Anthony may come to develop more confidence in the possibility of dealing with the ordinary oral aggression of ordinary mouths. During several sessions I have had to rescue farm animals from being devoured by implacable lions in order, as I said earlier, not to collude with what felt like the ethos of concentration camps; on each such occasion, he had at the end of the session "animals better". Mostly, however, this issue still appears as larger than life and as too frightening to tackle directly.

To summarize: For Anthony, the experience of separateness carried with it terrors about being dismembered and eaten, as well as extreme fears about the effect on his object of his oral aggression, which was easily confused with self-assertion. He attempted to circumvent these dangers—represented by a snapping mouth-like double structure that felt like separated parents re-uniting vengefully against him—by means of various devices. He might behave like a mutually adoring parental couple that excluded me; he might assert that he formed a threesome with the parents, indeed that he was the link between them; or he might clutch on to the drawstring of his tracksuit bottoms as though it offered the uninterrupted continuity of an umbilical cord that could protect him from a catastrophic psychological birth. Ringing the changes in terms of which aspect of the threesome of horse, shadow, and grass he was being at any given moment meant that his sense of identity remained highly unstable.

The relevance to patients with eating disorders

Patients with eating disorders can sometimes resort to some of these same self-protective strategies, although individuals vary in terms of which position of the tripartite structure of horse, shadow, and grass they predominantly occupy. They may also vary in terms of whether they think of themselves as being "between the parents", or whether they use food in a way similar to Anthony's "umbilical" drawstring—that is, in order to ward off the experience of separateness.

For example, a young woman came to treatment some years after suffering from quite severe anorexia during the time when her parents, who were separated, had been going through crises in their new relationships. She felt that she had been conceived in order to cement her parents' marriage, and that her mother had been depressed during her early childhood. This patient's ambition was to fit into clothes that she had worn before reaching sexual maturity. If we take seriously her idea of being the cement that bound her parents together (in terms of Anthony's scheme, the "glue" that held together the two components of the Face), then eliminating herself could be thought of as expressing both her wish to unite them and her wish to separate them. Occupying more space would necessarily force her parents apart, particularly if the space she occupied were that of a sexually mature woman. On the other hand, eliminating herself as the cement or glue would cause the marriage to fall apart.

McDougall's formerly anorexic patient Georgette, as I have mentioned, felt that she shared in the analyst's life to the extent of referring to "our" husband. McDougall (1989) suggested that Georgette behaved as though there were only one husband between her and her mother/analyst. She seems to have experienced herself as part of a threesome in which she and the analyst were two burgers "sharing" a pound coin, or a horse and shadow "sharing" the grass more equitably than Anthony seemed to think was possible, an arrangement that allowed her to circumvent in the transference the highly problematic relationship she had had with her mother. This delusional world view was resolved with the working-through of Georgette's sense of oral oedipal deprivation; before this, she had completely blanked out the existence of a sexual parental couple, although she had managed to get married herself and to train as a doctor.

An anorexic 9- to 15-year-old girl whom I have described elsewhere (Rhode, 1979) shared Georgette's apparent phantasy of there being only one life between two people—or, indeed, one of anything desirable. This girl, like Anthony, confused food with rival babies that were felt to leave no room for her inside a mother-figure. Birth for her meant being literally cut out of a "matrix". In reality, her mother had been concerned about the effect of another child on her marriage and had seriously considered a very late abortion; this was to be the fate of a number of later pregnancies. For a long time, this girl had an "unborn" quality, as though she kept herself in the position of the shadow. She seemed to feel that safety lay in repudiating sensuality and desire—"Gold kills", she said, "because everybody wants it."

In a similar vein, both MacLeod (1981) and the anorexic patient described by Rey (1994) seemed to turn away from food in order to exercise control over what felt to them like a destructive relationship with the mother or with both parents. This links with Williams's (1997) description of the use of the infant as a "receptacle" for maternal projections and her suggestion that a "no-entry" defence can be a means of keeping these out. Such projections would include the transgenerational factors first outlined by Fraiberg et al. (1975). As I have already mentioned, MacLeod needed to be pregnant—to contain an actual baby—in order to feel that she could expand above the 8-stone mark. This invites the speculation that she may have needed proof of being able to expand without killing a baby, as though she and a baby were horse and shadow. It is also possible that the condition of pregnancy may have felt similar to Anthony's position "between the parents" and thus allowed her to circumvent fears of mutual destructiveness (cannibalism) between the generations. These fears were also central to Tustin's treatment of a 13-year-old severely anorexic girl, who gained weight when the transference relationship was experienced as "good", involving endless mutual gratification (much as in Anthony's picture of a mutually adoring parental couple). This girl lost weight when the experience of frustration or limits led to a "bad" relationship in which patient and therapist lived at each other's expense. Deprivation, says Tustin (1958), led to the phantasy of "biting her way greedily into my body to take out the desirable supplies I had there (p. 194). "To decide to grow and to live meant draining her mother's resources" (p. 190).

Rey's patient (1994), for whom mother and baby were similarly locked in a mutually destructive relationship, seemed to feel it impossible to disentangle them by ordinary means, and she was tormented by the lack of a sense of her own identity. She resorted to the drastic device of starving "herself", which was supposed to kill the mother and free the baby. This again could be thought of as though the mother were the horse and the baby were the shadow. In Barrows's bulimic patient (1999), on the other hand, the sense of being a "shadow person" seemed at the beginning of treatment to embrace the whole of her personality, until the possibility of inhabiting the world of other human beings emerged during treatment.

Finally, I wish to mention a middle-aged woman who was obese rather than anorexic, and who had in the past suffered from alcohol abuse. This woman shared with my 19-year-old former anorexic patient the fear that she had caused her parents' marriage to break up by reaching puberty. She had had little experience of a supportive parental couple: her father had been in the army, so that she did not know him until she was nearly a year old, after which she felt that he intruded violently between her mother and her. Like the father of Barrows's patient, this father had suffered unmourned, traumatic bereavements. His means of asserting mastery over the threat of death seemed to be to insist on numerous abortions, with which his wife colluded. My patient, who as a young woman had attempted suicide when her mother told her about these abortions, had vivid memories of feeling lost in a terrifying blackness when her parents had left her in a residential nursery as a child. She attempted, not very successfully, to fend off the repetition of such experiences by means of relationships in which her partner was supposed to be always available, as though they formed a version of Anthony's "Mummy-and-Daddy" mirror-image. Her overeating and alcohol abuse could be seen as ways of denying separation—something like Anthony's umbilical cord. At the same time, she was equating herself with her father by being overweight and with her mother (who drank heavily when her husband left her) by means of her alcohol abuse. This calls to mind Anthony's equation of his skin to the skin of the Face.

Concluding remarks

I have attempted to illustrate similarities in the body image and sense of identity between a boy with autism who experienced eating as a highly destructive and dangerous function, and female patients with eating disorders. In each case, major difficulties (whether caused by maternal depression, transgenerational issues, or other factors) appear to have interfered with maternal mirroring of the baby's identity. In Tustin's terms (1981), psychological birth was experienced as psychological catastrophe: being a separate individual was experienced as highly dangerous, either to the persons themselves or to the parental couple and other children. Bodily integrity felt under threat, and the sense of identity appeared unstable or confused.

While my obese patient used food and alcohol to deny separateness, anorexic patients appeared instead to deny any bodily needs. Since food often seemed to be confused with rival babies who occupied the maternal object, taking in food could be misconstrued as being pushed out of forming a threesome with the parental couple. Anorexic patients' fears that eating will make them unattractive may be to do with feeling pushed out of the parents' sexual union into a state of bodily fragmentation and extreme vulnerability. Young (1996) has reported a similar reaction to the mental "food" of the analyst's words, which had to be fended off as they painfully exposed a "defective (wounded) surface".

In conclusion, it is obvious that crucial individual differences in these patients remain to be explored. Differing attitudes towards sensuous experience—which from Tustin and Meltzer onwards has been described as often serving anti-developmental purposes in children with autism—are likely to be crucial. So too is the proportion of the personality that is free to function outside the realms I have been concerned with here (Bion, 1957), and, within these realms, the degree of stability or rigidity in the adoption of any single coping strategy. It is my hope that thinking about Anthony's extreme predicament may be useful in understanding similar constellations in some adults with eating disorders.

CHAPTER SIX

Marco: a story of a school relationship

Maria Antionetta Catena

I have been working in a school in Rome for a number of years. The current class assigned to me comprises twenty 7-year-old children. The school timetable is organized around eight hours a day of work and play. I teach on alternate mornings and afternoons, four hours at a time, sharing the day with Anna, a colleague of mine. We do not work at weekends. A relationship of mutual esteem and friendship has developed between Anna and I. This has been partly facilitated by Anna and I attending a Tavistock-based course in Rome. Although Anna teaches Italian and I mathematics, we adopt similar values in our teaching approaches.

Meeting Marco

I met Marco before meeting the rest of the children, as he was introduced to me just before school officially began the new academic year. Marco was a pale-looking boy with a sweet face, a markedly hooked nose, and a tuft of blond hair. He was extremely thin and wore baggy trousers with a high waist. They were supported by braces, which made him look a little like Charlie Chaplin. On the first day of term, I found him standing in the hall alone by a door, gazing down. He was wearing new clothes and clutching the straps of his rucksack. I called to him by name, welcoming him and telling him that I would see him shortly. He had been the last one to arrive in the hall, where the children were being divided into classes. His mother was with him, and she pushed him towards his class group. Before she left, she whispered to me: "He was waiting in the classroom . . . he didn't realize that everyone was gathering in here." Marco lined up with the other children, and we went to the classroom. We all introduced ourselves to each other. Later the children began drawing, and the emotional impact of starting at school after the three-month summer holiday was clearly a powerful one. During the first break, Marco laid a placemat in front of him and began nibbling a small cake. All of a sudden he stood up and was sick. Anna took him by the hand to the bathroom, but he kept being sick in the corridor and then on the bathroom floor, making a mess of his new shoes and trousers. I remained with the rest of the children; there was an acrid smell in the air. The children all stopped eating: they seemed frozen and looked at me silently with serious, worried faces. Despite my having opened the windows, there was still a strong smell of vomit in the classroom. I joined Anna and Marco in the bathroom, where Anna had washed him and was now busy cleaning his shoes. Marco said to me that it was all right—this had often happened to him at nursery school. He drank a little water, and we went back together to the classroom. On his desk there was still his nibbled snack. I asked him what he wanted to do with it. He replied, "I shall take it home", and he then carefully folded up his placemat, put it in his rucksack, and sat quietly at his desk. He never once asked for his mother.

I remember a feeling of dismay at the violent and unpredictable vomiting that afflicted Marco, in such contrast to Marco's apparent resignation. It seemed just one in a long series of similar experiences he had got used to. In an effort to minimize the situation, his mother subsequently told me: "He has got used to it, you see, he doesn't attach any importance to it. At the nursery school he often used to be sick." Recurrent vomiting was a central feature of Marco's first months at school. It always came without any warning, when Marco was in the canteen, and it usually occurred before he began eating. I felt it was linked to an emotional experience that seemed to shake him as though stirred up by the environment he was now in. One day, as he had reached the canteen and before being sick, he began to stammer: "What a stench . . . what a stench." It appeared that some emotional experiences not sufficiently metabolized expressed themselves at a body level. Marco seemed to be ejecting something indigestible via an uncontrollable mechanism. At a meeting we had with the parents at the end of the year, the father remarked: "Marco has always vomited, even when he was small at home, not just at the nursery."

When Marco was not being sick in the canteen, he could eat virtually nothing. He repeated a series of obsessional rituals, which he tried to conceal, involving fiddling in front of the table with his head bent down. Grimly and with blank eyes, he would rub his plastic cutlery as if getting rid of some nasty residue. When finally making up his mind to face his food, he would turn the fork round on the table and cut up the food into tiny pieces, taking each one with the fork and staring at it suspiciously. He would put it in his mouth and quickly chew and swallow it. His approach to food seemed to indicate a certain difficulty in taking in and in biting, as if he were faced with having to deal with something toxic.

The Family

Marco had two older siblings who were approaching adolescence. His mother, an unassuming woman with an air of frailty, was about 40 years old. She had the appearance of a little girl and often blushed when I talked to her. When she talked she crossed her arms, her hands clutching her upper arms as though holding herself in, as if to contain an overwhelming emotion. The father—sturdy, unpretentious, and with a gentle, submissive air—was considerably older than the mother. The parents never came to see me together. The couple seemed to be going through a period of misunderstandings and sometimes open conflict. The mother stated that they disagreed on everything and spoke two different languages, not understanding each other. The father complained of violent scenes in which everyone in the family became involved. Aggression seemed to pervade family life, and the older children seemed to have formed an alliance against Marco. The father lamented the victimization of Marco, which he attributed to him being the youngest child. Marco's mother said that "When Marco is at home, he turns pale . . . his brothers mock him, they make him the butt of their jokes."

Both parents appeared to have had relatively deprived backgrounds. They seemed unwilling to discuss Marco's vomiting problems, which they brushed aside as though it had to be endured and had no remedy. The idea of psychological help was not one they would consider. Both parents conveyed a strong basic mistrust towards their own capacity to cope with their child's problem. They appeared to require the teachers to assume responsibility for dealing with threatening issues they themselves could not face. Despite much encouragement and effort, Marco was not referred for specialized help.

Marco in class

During his first months at school, Marco had frequent rows with the boy who sat next to him. This boy, Francesco, displayed obvious dislike and intolerance of Marco, preferring the company of other children. The two of them behaved spitefully to each other during lessons. For example, Francesco would reprimand Marco for trying to copy from his notebook: Marco would swallow this rebuke, his face drawn and twitching. Occasionally Marco would react by wrinkling his nose, showing his teeth, and contorting his features. However, often he could not react, seeming instead to choke with rage. Life was better for Marco when he was separated from Francesco, even though this produced isolation from the rest of the class. It was disconcerting to see that no one wanted to be with Marco; for his part, he never complained and seemed indifferent or resigned. His loneliness was obvious during playtime: instead of going out, he would often remain alone at his desk mumbling and gesticulating. Sometimes he walked obsessively up and down a specific route in the classroom while talking to himself.

Occasionally I asked him: "Marco, what are you doing?" "I am counting," he would reply, "I counted up to 750." If asked by me to join in with the other children, he would run over to them but not participate. After a short while he would find himself alone again, his head bent low. His odd behaviour, which, of course, was noticed by all his school mates and by my colleagues, filled me with dismay. He seemed to be consumed by a repetitive pattern from which there appeared to be no escape. During lessons, Marco was attentive, well behaved, and diligent. Over time he acquired the capacity to read and write in capital letters and became more questioning of his teachers. However, his interventions were often ill-timed, and he seemed restless and agitated, as though needing to draw attention to himself. It gradually emerged that Marco was a gifted child and one of the most able in his class. His ability to observe intelligently and grasp complex situations was impressive. He was pleased when praised about his work, blushing slightly, but his inhibitions did not stop him from becoming a model for other children, especially in the area of reading. His talents evoked a degree of astonishment in many people, as they contrasted so sharply with his odd behaviour. Gradually his admiring school mates came to view him as a "special child", as though he belonged to a different dimension from normal human life. When speaking from the front of the class, Marco appeared wise, ordered, and thoughtful. It was as though Marco was trying to become absorbed in a world of words and knowledge, which I thought might protect him from his more distressing inner world of feelings. He had somehow hardened himself by creating a "second skin" that was able to shield him from the misfortunes of life.

Marco's communications through drawing

After lunch the children often engaged in drawings, and they presented their finished work to their teacher for discussion. Marco's work was not beautiful, but it was quickly executed and seemed to reflect Marco's internal world. His initial drawings were stereotyped, revealing a numbed child who expressed himself in an infantile way by drawing birds, the sun, and little houses.

However, Marco's birds were drawn in the form of a squadron: each bird was a sharp triangular shape containing eyes and a beak. They looked bizarre and had worried human faces. Dangerous-looking birds preoccupied Marco for some time. Gradually, he took to drawing boats at sea, which themselves were shaped like the birds—triangular and sharp—but they were supported by the waves, which seemed rather like containers. The waves were rounded and occasionally sharp, and both the birds and the boats seemed to have a penetrating quality to them. After the birds and boats came little houses, occasionally with trees and woods around them. In one drawing there were some birds in the centre of the picture and two houses—a small and a large one—were on opposite sides of the drawing, divided by a long line of pointed blades of grass (Figure 1). The worrying, threatening birds were held at bay in the sky while the houses, kept separate, appeared quiet and peaceful. In subsequent drawings, the houses became taller or no longer straight, giving the impression of fragility. Later, windows were added that looked like eyes, and smoke emerged from inside the house. This evolved into an "ogre's" house, which Marco

FIGURE 1 Birds descending into a field

repeated over and over again. Fragile, ramshackle houses were, I think, Marco's way of conveying his *experience* of a fragile and precarious object who could not offer access. Marco's desires seemed to have been turned into a terrible rage against this impervious object. He wanted to penetrate and attack the object—hence the sharp and pointed birds and boats. I wondered whether the drawings of the ogre's house, which frightened Marco so much, could represent the possible transformation of attacking impulses that came back to persecute Marco.

Marco's verbal communications and the appearance of the policeman

Marco's odd behaviour and recurrent vomiting were a source of great anxiety to me and to others. I did my best to stay with him when he was being sick, but I often felt I might not be able to manage it. While cleaning him up, I would talk to him in order to try to understand what was taking place. Marco's comments were strange: for example, he said: "I like tortellini . . . but you see, there is this policeman." In response to my quizzical look, Marco pointed to his throat: "Yes, he is here. He is like this . . .", and Marco raised his arm as if to portray a steel bar. I asked Marco whether the policeman prevented food from going down. "No", he calmly explained, "it brings back what I have swallowed." I suggested that we really must find a way of sending this policeman away. Marco smiled faintly, raising his arm and saying: "It's like that even when I am asleep." This odd, rather intense conversation gave a glimpse of something of Marco's complex inner world. Things became more complicated as Marco subsequently revealed that the policeman had split into two different versions, which then multiplied into a host of "little little policemen" that lodged in his throat and did not permit him to retain food. Marco came across as persecuted and full of shame: he referred to the little policemen as though they were an unmentionable secret that no one should discover.

Having communicated his distress to me via his vomiting and the "little policemen", Marco at one point drew three houses en-

FIGURE 2 The "worst war". A drawing depicting a throwing game between the members of Marco's family

shrouded in smoke. He brought the drawing to show me and explained excitedly that the smoke was "entangled, here, you see?" He traced wisps of smoke with his fingertip, indicating how they entwined with the smoke coming out of the other houses. I asked another child whether he had finished his drawing about the war, and Marco immediately intervened, saying: "There is always a war at home, they quarrel all the time, they throw things at each other, they throw everything . . ." (Figure 2). Marco continued to produce regular drawings of houses from which smoke emanated (Figure 3), and these houses got bigger and bigger until they were touching the sky. He repeated the same theme constantly: he drew small and big houses with smoke pouring out from the inside, through the roof, and spreading out into the space beyond. Spirals of smoke, entwined together, permeated everything. I had the impression that he was indicating an emotional experience related to objects or people that give out or eject from the inside. There seemed to be no container, no means by which things could be taken in, including, I felt, Marco's projections. The emissions of smoke that Marco drew seemed to have a lethal aspect. "The sun coughs", he explained, "because it got intoxicated." As Marco developed his theme of big, smoking houses, so his drawings acquired an increasingly confused quality, as though composed of a seething magma of indistinct elements. He talked with me about these drawings in earnest detail, as though desperate to be listened to—to have someone who would take all the smoke without coughing or becoming intoxicated. Gradually I came to understand that Marco had no internalized object capable of receiving his projections and giving a meaning to his feelings. Like his first self-portrait, showing a child with a huge hand used for clinging or gripping, I felt that Marco had me in his grip, desperately monitoring and checking my reactions to see if I had accepted and understood him, and whether I could withstand the impact of his communications.

Allowing himself to be understood was not easy for Marco. He would divide his sheet of drawing paper into four sections in order to tell his story. There would be, for example, a child who spoke English, then a teacher-mother who did not understand the child,

FIGURE 3 An exchange of smoke between houses

and then the teacher-mother telling the child to be quiet, and finally a picture of the teacher-mother at home quarrelling with her husband. Through these demarcated segments, Marco communicated the nature of his relationship to the parental objects. Mother and son speak different languages: they do not communicate or understand each other, and he is left with rage and feelings of being misunderstood, and having no space or place in his mother's mind. Parents are only perceived as "making hatred" not "making love". In subsequent drawings, Marco developed the theme of the conflict with his mother and his father and of the alliance of his brothers against him. One drawing depicted a "drizzle of little letters" that circled in the air above Marco's and his brothers' heads. "They have torn each other's faces, they all went mad with the smell of the chicken in the oven." These little letters have no links to each other or anything else and cannot be utilized for thinking, only for evacuation. (This is reminiscent of Bion's beta-elements: Bion, 1962.) It is possible that they were echoes of primary experiences in Marco, reflecting a distress that was never recognized or contained. Marco's profound, unremitting loneliness was becoming clearer. It was expressed in a tragic story that he wrote in class, about a child on Mars.

The child who lives on Mars

The story begins: "Once upon a time there was a child who lived on Mars. One day he decided to make a journey by spaceship through the solar system. By mistake he ended up in another galaxy and lost his star maps. The child thought he knew these maps by heart and continued his journey but found himself on an alien satellite and crashed. He had to rebuild the spaceship but ran out of money when he got to the nose. He therefore had to stay on the satellite planet but over time he got used to it."

We can see how Marco is touching on the theme of his yearning for an object perceived as vital for survival, but also out of reach. One can suppose that the story reflects something of his primary relationship with the maternal object, and his anxieties about how to approach the object. He may be avoiding reaching it in order to preserve it from terrible attacks. Perhaps the penetrating nose of the spaceship with its sharp point and which Marco could not repair indicates a return to an earlier theme of "penetrating" his object, breaking and entering it, the consequences of which he may experience as disastrous. The story of the child who lived on Mars was produced towards the end of Marco's first year at school, from which point on he began to write prolifically and more articulately. During this year at school, Marco had introduced the central threads of his problems and communicated a desperate need for someone receptive and ready to accept his outpourings and to accurately understand them. He struggled to symbolize his persecuting experiences by referring to the "little policeman" that gave form to a feeling that upset him. I recall one drawing of houses with smoke to which he then added vivid colours: the plumes of smoke became intertwined with colourful threads resembling streamers.

My colleague Anna and I tried to relate to Marco, providing him with an experience of being taken seriously. We were encouraged by the fact that by the end of the school year his episodes of vomiting had become less frequent. There were also moments when he would walk hand-in-hand with us, perhaps indicating that we had made his loneliness a little more tolerable.

Second grade—during and after the summer break

At the end of the summer holiday Marco's mother told me that Marco was eager to get back to school. She also said that the relationship between Marco and one of his brothers had worsened. We had received a postcard from Marco with the caption: "Ladispoli; charm and mystery." We were amused by this card because Ladispoli is a rather dull seaside resort in an unattractive landscape. We wondered whether the "charm and mystery" was Marco's attempt to ensure that we remained thinking of him, and that he was not forgotten.

The second school year got under way and we were struck by the fact that Marco was only sick once in the canteen during this entire year. It happened early on, perhaps as a result of the emotional turmoil of returning to school after a break. Although his sickness had ceased, I became more and more concerned by his difficulties around eating, which were increasingly evident at meal times. Marco's mother confirmed these difficulties by describing how Marco would clean his cutlery after each mouthful so that meals seemed to take forever. He would request special dishes and then refuse to eat at all. Marco's paediatrician reported that he had lost 9 pounds in weight and prescribed a tonic, which Marco took for a while. Marco referred to his food as "good for me but poison for other people". His approach to food seemed to be full of aggression and was similar to the relationship with the maternal object, described earlier. One day he confided that he could not eat because "in the canteen there are two children who look at me . . . they are suspicious . . .". Later he sketched these children in the form of soldier-like creatures holding bloodstained daggers. These figures were pointed and adorned by medals and decorations, with bloodstained knives and swords all around them. The drawing seemed to confirm that Marco, when eating, was beset by terrible persecutory phantasies. He seemed to experience moments in which all the sharp and cutting elements of eating came into play—teeth, fork, knife. They seemed to become aggressive objects, which could wound and rip. As a result, the attacked food became poisonous and lethal. Perhaps because of such terrible phantasies Marco was avoiding being in contact with food as much as he could, trying to delay his meals through various strategies and obsessional rituals. As the year went on, the time he took to eat grew longer and longer and his actions became slower. He always found that he needed something before he could begin eating: for example, "I don't have any cutlery" . . . "I was not given the first course . . .", etc. Sometimes we suggest that children with eating difficulties bring their own sandwiches, which they often find preferable to school food. Marco seemed to prefer eating home-made sandwiches and gave the impression that biting into the bread calmed him down. We wondered whether eating his own food made the food less toxic in his mind, and whether our encouragement to eat in this way might enable him to face his disturbing feelings.

Communicating and not communicating: conversations during breaks at school

Marco also became more able to conduct a one-to-one conversation during his second year at school. During both terms, Marco and I or Anna (the other teacher) would often go out onto the terrace to talk, and he was able to communicate the intensity of his distress. At the same time we noticed that his way of speaking seemed to have acquired a wish to mislead the listener. He could produce unintelligible sounds or at times talk as though pretending to communicate. Sometimes he moved his lips without making any sound and then laughed at the misunderstandings caused. I had the impression that he was trying to secure even greater attention from me, to exert more control over my ability to bear his distress, and to test my reactions to him. By talking for long enough with him, we gradually established better contact. For example, he would wander up and down the terrace in search of "enemies . . . because there is a war . . . and the war is not only the one in Iraq". On another occasion, he told me of how he had peeped through the keyhole of a door on the terrace, which is always locked. He had seen "a hand with nails as long as claws, wandering around in a smoke-like haze". He said that he had discovered niches in the wall where enemies kept their weapons. There were enemies everywhere, he said, and he had several arms depots to defend himself. "The enemies can attack my home but I have set traps for them", he said. After sharing these persecutory phantasies he whispered: "Do you know what's nice when these things happen? You and Anna call me over and we can talk about them together."

Written communications

The second year of school seemed to be the year of the stories for Marco. The symbolic value of learning and of mastering the techniques of written language became more meaningful to him. He attained outstanding results. His wish to use learning in order to understand became apparent, as if he were determined to strengthen his capacity for insight. "I hope to be able to understand more when we study the revolutions", he whispered to me one day at the end of a conversation in which he had talked about enemies and the war he was forced to fight all the time. His first significant written story began after the Christmas break and after a period in December when Anna had been away and had been replaced by a locum. His earliest stories entitled "Mr Cheat" and "The Flight of the Animals" were characterized by the absence of loving or protecting objects, no salvation, and nothing but the repetition of difficult situations that were never resolved. One could see the recurrent appearance of misleading elements in the stories, usually represented by characters producing misunderstanding and false statements. There was no safety. When Marco wrote of the flight of the animals from the zoo to freedom, which heralded a happy ending, the reader was left with anxiety about the consequences of uncontained animals such as tigers and giraffes mixing with one another. Marco's dexterity with language was considerable, and he excelled through his ability to change the terms of a story into their opposites. Changing the context of a story and arriving at new meanings created much excitement in him and placed his school mates in a puzzling situation. It was as though Marco was never satisfied in his pursuit of new meanings and interpretations, and as a result he continually broke the established links that tied him to others. His mode of speaking was not designed to communicate, but, rather, to hide behind. Whatever the nature of the underlying conflicts that beset Marco, he had evolved a form of pseudo-communication to defend against these. These consisted of an intermingling of truth with lies, in a bewildering tangle that left others confused.

The novel and the map

After the Christmas holiday and during the month of February, Marco produced a "novel" that he wrote at home. He had much earlier informed us that he would like to be a writer of detective stories when he grew up, and he had already begun practising. One morning, Marco arrived at school carrying a plastic carrier-bag and handed it to me without saying a word. There was a lot of activity taking place in the classroom at the same time; another pupil, Claudia, was trying to give me a bag containing two goldfish. I remarked briefly to Marco: "Are these your drawings? Well done! I'll look at them later." Marco stared at me looking upset, while around us the excitement grew as we were urged to watch the two goldfish. Later that afternoon I realized that Marco had given me his "novel". It was a detective story in nine chapters and totalled forty-two pages. The story centred on the search for a valuable picture that had been stolen from an artist. The narrative was hard to follow because of its pressing rhythm, which confused the sequence of events taking place. The reader easily lost track of the story. Stylistically the story was constructed using suspense and sudden changes, the purpose of which seemed to be to exert control over the reader. Marco's father had commented: "The story kept me on the edge of my seat. I held my breath until the last minute!" Within the plot were confused and contradictory elements such as bad guys who looked like good guys, and situations in which characters received information that they believed, only to find themselves misled and cheated. There was a type of speech from the characters which reminded me of Marco's need to get rid of something that he could not contain (as in the drawings of houses and smoke). It was possible to perceive an anxiety in Marco to regain the desired object, "the valuable picture", despite the characters of the story never choosing to help. Marco produced a map for me—this would have taken me on a long, tortuous, and confusing journey, at the end of which I had to use a tiny boat if I were to fulfil my goal. As Marco indicated the route my little boat would take, he seemed amused and increasingly excited and confused as potential disasters threatened me. "Will you find the treasure in the end? Look at what is going to happen to you. This is the island of the logs. . . . Yes, yes, you will find the treasure. . . ." The route Marco mapped out for me was full of dangers such as erupting volcanoes, whales, ships that could bombard me with gunfire, islands on fire.

The map was linked to the content of Marco's novel in that both were concerned with the impossibility of reaching a treasured object due to persistent obstacles and multiple misunderstandings. The theme of misunderstanding, of one person not understanding another, played a central role and reminded me of Marco's earlier drawings in which he portrayed mother and child as speaking two different languages. Marco seemed to be reproducing a relationship to an internal maternal object interfered with by many misunderstandings. These misunderstandings had the effect of undermining the attempts to reach the "treasure"; in other words, the main character was prevented from establishing a good and enduring relationship with a longed-for object. Wandering around serves also to prevent an approach to the object, probably to preserve it from ferocious attacks. Marco talks in the novel about a "run-down house, in fact a destroyed castle that was smashed after a revolution". Wandering around incessantly also prevented Marco from being taken in and "eaten" and thereby destroyed.

The novel and the map seemed to portray the fullness of Marco's aggression and rage but also a very worrying excitement that he felt in playing a destructive game of blindly wandering around. Although this defensive activity may have held him together and protected him from risk of disintegration, the satisfaction he felt in multiplying the obstacles in this way seemed to increase feelings of exclusion. In this phantasy world, he became lost in a state of mind that paid little interest to contact with the real world. A crucial mitigating factor in all of this was the importance that Marco attributed to his relationship with me and with Anna. This, together with the striking symbolic quality of his creations, provided some hope for the future.

The beginnings of a process of elaboration

In early spring of the second year, Marco stayed away from school for a few days due to a bad headache caused by a complete loss of appetite. Marco felt unwell and vomited in the parents' car. We wondered whether his illness related to emotional distress converted into bodily expression. This time appeared to be one of great disturbance for Marco, but also a turning point. While he was unwell, he received a great deal of attention from his mother, and he was thoroughly checked by a very caring paediatrician, the combined effect of this, along with a warm welcome from us when he came back to school, being like the infusion of new life-blood for him. Once back at school, Marco began to write more directly autobiographical stories in which the interferences disrupting the communication had diminished drastically. The appearance of sincere, genuine feelings and experiences in his stories gave rise to more lively, sympathetic, and emotionally expressive narratives. One story, "The Greedy Ant", helped us understand something of the dynamics and the communications between Marco, Anna, and myself. One lunchtime I noticed Marco fiddling with his fork and holding his head in his hands. He had eaten nothing, but I left him in the canteen while the second sitting for lunch took place, in the hope that he might manage to eat. When he eventually arrived back in class, I asked him how much he had been eating, and he said "Zero!" in a provocative manner. I was worried about his loss of appetite, especially after his recent illness. I took him to one side and gave him a little talk on the importance of eating in order to grow and be healthy. He made a face at me, but also seemed to be pleased about my concern. I suggested that we go together to the canteen and ask for a sandwich for him. He replied that he would like a cheese sandwich, but then in his usual misleading way began to move his lips and to smile in an attempt to create a misunderstanding between us. I cut this short and took him down to the canteen, where I was told that there was only a ham sandwich available. Marco was given his sandwich and we returned to the classroom, but before we left the canteen I noticed that Marco was eating his sandwich with apparent enjoyment, something that took me greatly by surprise. A little later in the classroom, he brought me his empty plate and said, "Teacher, I have finished", with a happy look on his face. The following day I read Marco's first draft of his new story.

"The Greedy Ant"

> Once upon a time a family of ants lived behind a blackboard in a school room. These ants were quite aristocratic and wore elegant red dresses decorated with white, soft plumes. One of them was extremely greedy, and as soon as someone said "breadcrumbs" it immediately rushed out to get some. However, the other ants prevented it from leaving the nest, saying

that there was a terrible black monster outside with pointed teeth—in fact, this was the blackboard. A party was organized in the ants' nest, with sandwiches and twenty cakes. The greedy ant, instead of making merry with the others, took advantage of the confusion to sneak out and look for something better elsewhere, such as 30,000 boxes of pastries filled with cream or chocolate. But when the ant left the nest, instead of finding the 30,000 boxes of chocolate and cream pastries, it came across a huge black monster with rows of sharp teeth. On one side the monster held a big stick attached to a chain with a round thing at the end with blood stains. The ant turned white with fear—as white as a breadcrumb—and fell on the floor. Another ant who was inside the ants' nest making merry noticed this breadcrumb (which was actually the ant) and looked around for the greedy ant to prevent it from going out for the breadcrumb. Not finding the greedy ant, it thought that it must have gone out to the breadcrumb, which placed the friendly ant in a quandary. "Should I go out or should I not? It is better to go out. I can't leave my friend in trouble, real friends don't do that." Eventually, after much vacillation, it sneaked out of the ant's nest and noticed that the breadcrumb had the greedy ant's face. The friendly ant tried to make the greedy ant recover consciousness but failed. Half an hour later the greedy ant seemed to recover and stuttered, "The black monster", and the friendly ant answered in a loud voice, "You see what happens when you disobey?" The greedy ant ran away, not listening to the words of its friend, and when it eventually stopped it looked round and wasn't scared any more. It was happy, there were lots of new things around, including stripes on a white sky and plenty of red, blue, and green numbers and large and beautiful drawings of different kinds. The only things that seemed to be missing were breadcrumbs and 30,000 boxes of cream and chocolate pastries, so the greedy ant went on looking for something good to eat until it came across something that looked very pretty—orange and grey with pink on top. The greedy ant climbed on top of it in search of the 30,000 boxes of cream and chocolate pastries, and after climbing a long way it found a lot of breadcrumbs. The greedy ant ate them and went back to the nest. On the way back it noticed that the black monster was only a blackboard because there were maths exercises written on it and the pointed teeth were squares drawn in chalk, and the stick on a chain was the support that held up the blackboard, and the stain of blood on the round thing was only red chalk on the duster. The greedy ant went back home to the ant's nest and told his friends all about his adventure.

Discussion

This story represented, in my view, a step forward for Marco as it involved some working through of persecutory anxieties. He seemed to be working on the differences between phantasy and reality. Marco seemed to be facing squarely his problems with food for the first time and was identifying the nature of the persecutory object that gripped him. A terrible greed, a frantic search for ever better things, lay behind his conflictual relationship with food. This aggressive greed terrified him and probably prevented him from eating. In phantasy, he seemed to equate devouring with being devoured. In this skilfully created story, it seemed that Marco was in genuine contact with a very frightening part of himself, and at the same time it demonstrated confidence in his own ability to overcome his terror. It was also the first occasion when he explicitly revealed enjoyment of the nice things around him. The fact that the story was set in a classroom similar to his own was also encouraging. It seemed reasonable to hope that Marco might find, instead of the idealized 30,000 boxes of cream and chocolate pastries, some good, fresh, nourishing bread instead. A separate source of encouragement was the way in which Marco joyfully shared this story with others. He seemed to be experiencing a sense of being understood—confidence or hope that his anxieties would be contained and tolerated. These conditions helped him to metabolize some of his painful feelings and fostered a process of improvement.

Marco's story of the greedy ant affected Anna and I deeply. It was a moving experience when the three of us discussed together the adventures of the little ant. Marco's eyes shone with pleasure rather than excitement, and he gave the impression that he had finally come out of his dark loneliness. It became apparent that despite the many difficulties of communication and the critical moments we had experienced during our time with Marco, school nevertheless seemed to have been an experience that Marco valued deeply. Central to this in my opinion was Marco's relationship with his teachers, which represented an important foundation for the resumption of aspects of his development. The level of attachment he showed to us indicated that he had made a great investment in his relationship with us—literally so—as it was now often difficult for us to free ourselves of his hugs. Sometimes, while I was drinking coffee, Marco would now come and plant kisses on my cheek, whispering "I don't even let you have your coffee". At the end of school days he now sent sets of vital messages designed to convey his feelings about the imminent separation. "I am struck by acute teacher sickness!" he would confide to me, while giving me a kiss. "When I get to the fifth grade, what shall I do then?" he asked very seriously on the last day of the school year. I suggested that the children draw a scene from *The Magic Flute* by Mozart. During the previous year we had seen Bergman's film of the opera, and it had inspired our art classes. Marco was the first to produce a drawing. The scene was somewhat disheartening, a wasteland where only bare trees grew. Frighteningly, Papageno, the bird-catcher, is hanging himself on a tree. I was alarmed and asked Marco to tell me what was happening in the drawing. He explained that Papagena, his girlfriend, had disappeared. I asked Marco what was going to happen. He replied: "Papageno will be saved by the angels (the three genies) and then Papagena will come back, but he doesn't know it yet." I replied: "Poor Papageno, he must be distraught." Marco nodded: "Yes, he is!" Marco had chosen the central theme of Papageno's despair, located between two happy moments, to convey his profound unhappiness and feeling of abandonment and loss at our forthcoming separation. I suggested to Marco: "Shall we give poor Papageno some hope that someone will come?" "Yes, without the angels arriving", Marco promptly answered. We continued to discuss Papageno's plight, and I was left with the memory of Marco planting kisses on my face and the feelings he needed to communicate of despair about separation.

REFERENCES

Alvarez, A. (1992). *Love's Company: Psychoanalytic Psychotherapy with Autistic, Borderline, Deprived and Abused Children*. London: Routledge.

Alvarez, A. (2000). Borderline children: Differentiating disturbance and deficit. In: M. Rustin & E. Quagliata (Eds.), *Assessment in Child Psychotherapy* (pp. 33–50). Tavistock Clinic Series. London: Duckworth.

Barrows, K. (1999). Ghosts in the swamp: Some aspects of splitting and their relationship to parental losses. *International Journal of Psycho-Analysis, 80*: 549–561.

Barrows, P. (2000). The use of stories as autistic objects. *Journal of Child Psychotherapy, 27*: 69–82.

Bick, E. (1964). Notes on infant observation in psycho-analytic training. *International Journal of Psycho-Analysis, 45*: 558–566.

Bick, E. (1968). The experience of the skin in early object relations. *International Journal of Psycho-Analysis, 49*: 484–486.

Bick, E. (1986). Further contributions on the function of the skin in early object relations. *British Journal of Psychotherapy, 2*: 292–299.

Bion, W. R. (1950). The imaginary twin. In: *Second Thoughts: Selected*

Papers on Psycho-Analysis (pp. 3–22). London: Heinemann, 1967. Reprinted London: Karnac, 1984.

Bion, W. R. (1957). Differentiation of the psychotic from the non-psychotic personalities. In: *Second Thoughts: Selected Papers on Psycho-Analysis* (pp. 43–64). London: Heinemann, 1967. Reprinted London: Karnac, 1984.

Bion, W. R. (1958). Attacks on linking. *International Journal of Psycho-Analysis, 40*: 308–315. Also in: *Second Thoughts: Selected Papers on Psycho-Analysis* (pp. 93–109). London: Heinemann, 1967. Reprinted London: Karnac, 1984.

Bion, W. R. (1962). *Learning from Experience*. London: Heinemann. Reprinted London: Karnac, 1984.

Birksted-Breen, D. (1989). Working with an anorexic patient. *International Journal of Psycho-Analysis, 77*: 29–40.

Boris, H. (1984). The problem of anorexia nervosa. *International Journal of Psycho-Analysis, 65*: 315–22.

Bott-Spillius, E. (1993). Varieties of envious experience. *International Journal of Psycho-Analysis, 74*: 1199–1212.

Briggs, S. (1993). *Psychological Insights from Infants with Eating Disorders*. Tavistock Clinic Paper, No. 135.

Briggs, S. (1997). *Growth and Risk in Infancy*. London: Jessica Kingsley.

Britton, R. (1989). The missing link: Parental sexuality in the Oedipus complex. In: J. Steiner (Ed.), *The Oedipus Complex Today* (pp. 83–101). London: Karnac.

Britton, R. (1998). Subjectivity, objectivity and triangular space. In: *Belief and Imagination: Explorations in Psychoanalysis* (pp. 41–58). New Library of Psychoanalysis. London & New York: Routledge.

di Cagno, L. (1984). "Early Mother–Baby Relationship, in the Light of Mother's Fantasies during Pregnancy, Circumstances of Birth, and Inborn Capacities of the Baby." Paper delivered at the Tavistock Clinic, London.

Earnshaw, A. (1994). Autism: A family affair? *Journal of Child Psychotherapy, 20*: 85–102.

Fraiberg, S., Adelson, E., & Shapiro, V. (1975). Ghosts in the nursery: A psychoanalytic approach to the problem of impaired infant–mother relationships. *Journal of the American Academy of Child Psychiatry, 14*: 387–422. Reprinted in S. Fraiberg (Ed.), *Clinical Studies in Infant Mental Health*. London: Tavistock, 1980.

Freud, S. (1909). Notes upon a case of obsessional neurosis. *S.E., 10*: 153–249.

Freud, S. (1917). Mourning and melancholia. *S.E., 14*: 243–258.

Freud, S. (1919). A child is being beaten: A contribution to the study of the origin of sexual perversions. *S.E., 17*: 7–122.

Haag, G. (1985). La mère et le bébé dans les deux moitiés du corps. *Neuropsychiatrie de l'Enfance, 33*: 107–114.

Haag, G. (1991). Nature de quelques identifications dans l'image du corps. *Journal de la Psychanalyse de l'Enfant, 9*: 73–92.

Klauber, T. (1999). The significance of trauma and other factors in work with the parents of children with autism. In: A. Alvarez & S. Reid (Eds.), *Autism and Personality: Findings from the Tavistock Autism Workshop* (pp. 33–48). London & New York: Routledge.

Klein, H. S. (1985). A Kleinian point of view. *Journal of Child Psychotherapy, 2* (2): 31–47.

Klein, M. (1932). *The Psycho-Analysis of Children. The Writings of Melanie Klein, Vol. 2*. London: Hogarth Press, 1975.

Klein, M. (1946). Notes on some schizoid mechanisms. In: *The Writings of Melanie Klein, Vol. 3: Envy and Gratitude and Other Works* (pp. 1–24). London: Hogarth Press, 1975.

Klein, M. (1952). On observing the behaviour of young infants. In: *The Writings of Melanie Klein, Vol. 3: Envy and Gratitude and Other Works* (pp. 94–121). London: Hogarth Press, 1975.

Klein, M. (1955). On identification. In: *The Writings of Melanie Klein, Vol. 3: Envy and Gratitude and Other Works* (pp. 141–175). London: Hogarth Press, 1975.

Klein, M. (1957). Envy and gratitude. In: *The Writings of Melanie Klein, Vol. 3: Envy and Gratitude and Other Works* (pp. 176–235). London: Hogarth Press, 1975.

Klein, S. (1980). Autistic phenomena in neurotic patients. *International Journal of Psycho-Analysis, 61*: 395–402. Also in: J. S. Grotstein (Ed.), *Do I Dare Disturb the Universe?* (pp. 103–113) Beverly Hills, CA: Caesura Press, 1981.

Lawrence, M. (2001). Loving them to death: The anorexic and her objects. *International Journal of Psycho-Analysis, 82*: 43–45.

Likierman, M. (1997). On rejection: Adolescent girls and anorexia. *Journal of Child Psychotherapy, 23*: 61–80.

MacLeod, S. (1981). *The Art of Starvation*. London: Virago.

Magagna, J. (2000). Severe eating difficulties: Attacks on life. In: M. Rustin & E. Quagliata (Eds.), *Assessment in Child Psychotherapy* (pp. 59–73). Tavistock Clinic Series. London: Duckworth.

McDougall, J. (1989). *Theatres of the Body*. London: Free Association Books.

Meltzer, D. (1974). Adhesive identification. In: *Sincerity and Other Works: Collected Papers of Donald Meltzer* (pp. 335–350), ed. A. Hahn. London: Karnac, 1994.

Meltzer, D. (1986). The conceptual distinction between projective identification and container-contained. In: *Studies in Extended Metapsychology* (pp. 50–69). Strathtay: Clunie Press.

Meltzer, D., Bremner, J., Hoxter, H., Weddell, D., & Wittenberg, I. (1975). *Explorations in Autism*. Strathtay: Clunie Press.

Miller, L., Rustin, M., Rustin, M. J., & Shuttleworth, J. (Eds.) (1989). *Closely Observed Infants*. London: Duckworth.

Money-Kyrle, R. (1971). The aim of psycho-analysis. *International Journal of Psycho-Analysis, 52*: 103–106. Also in: *The Collected Papers of Roger Money-Kyrle* (pp. 442–449). Strathtay: Clunie Press, 1978.

O'Shaughnessy, E. (1964). The absent object. *Journal of Child Psychotherapy, 1* (2).

O'Shaughnessy, E. (1981). A clinical study of a defensive organisation. *International Journal of Psycho-Analysis, 62*: 359–369.

O'Shaughnessy, E. (1999). Relating to the superego. *International Journal of Psycho-Analysis*, *80*: 861–870.

Palazzoli, M. S. (1963). *Self-Starvation: From the Intrapsychic to the Transpersonal Approach to Anorexia Nervosa*. London: Human Content Books, 1974.

Raphael-Leff, J. (1991). *Psychological Processes of Childbearing*. London: Chapman & Hall.

Reid, S. (1999). Autism and trauma: Autistic post-traumatic developmental disorder. In: A. Alvarez & S. Reid (Eds.), *Autism and Personality: Findings from the Tavistock Autism Workshop* (pp. 93–112). London & New York: Routledge.

Rey, H. (1988). That which patients bring to analysis. In: *Universals of Psychoanalysis in the Treatment of Psychotic and Borderline States (The Collected Papers of Henri Rey)* (pp. 229–248), ed. J. Magagna. London: Free Association Books, 1994.

Rey, H. (1994). Anorexia nervosa. In: *Universals of Psychoanalysis in the Treatment of Psychotic and Borderline States (The Collected Papers of*

Henri Rey) (pp. 47–75), ed. J. Magagna. London: Free Association Books, 1994.

Rhode, E. (1994). *Psychotic Metaphysics* (Chaps. 5, 6). London: Karnac.

Rhode, M. (1979). One life between two people: Some themes from the analysis of a nine-to-fifteen-year-old anorexic girl. *Journal of Child Psychotherapy. 5*: 57–68.

Rhode, M. (1999). Echo or answer? The move towards ordinary speech in three children with autistic spectrum disorder. In: A. Alvarez & S. Reid (Eds.), *Autism and Personality: Findings from the Tavistock Autism Workshop.* London & New York: Routledge.

Rhode, M. (2000). On using an alphabet: Recombining separable components. In: J. Symington (Ed.), *Imprisoned Pain: A Festschrift for H. Sydney Klein* (pp. 80–97). London: Karnac.

Rhode, M. (2002). One life between two people: The relation of autistic anxieties to themes from the analysis of a nine-to-fifteen year-old anorexic girl. In: E. Quagliata (Ed.), *Un bisogno vitale.* Rome: Astrolabio, 2002.

Rosenbluth, D. (1965). The Kleinian theory of depression. *Journal of Child Psychotherapy, 1* (3): 20–25.

Rosenfeld, H. (1987). *Impasse and Interpretation.* London: Tavistock.

Rustin, M., Rhode, M., Dubinsky, A., & Dubinsky, H. (Eds.) (1997). *Psychotic States in Children.* London: Routledge.

Steiner, J. (1993). *Psychic Retreats: Pathological Organizations in Psychotic, Neurotic and Borderline Patients.* New Library of Psychoanalysis. London: Routledge.

Symington, J. (1985). The survival function of primitive omnipotence. *International Journal of Psycho-Analysis, 66*: 481–486.

Tischler, S. (1979). Being with a psychotic child: A psycho-analytical approach to the problems of parents with psychotic children. *International Journal of Psycho-Analysis, 60*: 29–38.

Tustin, F. (1958). Anorexia nervosa in an adolescent girl. *British Journal of Medical Psychology, 31*: 184–200.

Tustin, F. (1972). *Autism and Childhood Psychosis.* London: Hogarth Press.

Tustin, F. (1981). Psychological birth and psychological catastrophe. In: *Autistic States in Children* (revised edition, pp. 96–110). London: Routledge, 1992. Also in: J. S. Grotstein (Ed.), *Do I Dare Disturb the Universe?* (pp. 181–196). Beverly Hills, CA: Caesura Press, 1981.

Tustin, F. (1986). *Autistic Barriers in Neurotic Patients.* London: Karnac.

Tustin, F. (1990). *The Protective Shell in Children and Adults*. London: Karnac.

Tustin, F. (1994). The perpetuation of an error. *Journal of Child Psychotherapy, 20*: 3–23.

Williams, G. (1997). *Internal Landscapes and Foreign Bodies: Eating Disorders and Other Pathologies*. Tavistock Clinic Series. London: Duckworth.

Williams, G., & Judd, D. (2002). *International Journal of Infant Observation and Its Application*, *5* (2).

Winnicott, D. W. (1960). String: A technique of communication. In: *The Maturational Processes and the Facilitating Environment* (pp. 153–157). London: Hogarth Press, 1965. Reprinted London: Karnac, 1990.

Winnicott, D. W. (1967). Mirror-role of mother and family in child development. In: *Playing and Reality* (pp. 111–118). London & New York: Tavistock/Routledge, 1971.

Wittenberg, I. (1975). Primal depression in autism—John. In: D. Meltzer, J. Bremner, H. Hoxter, D. Weddell, & I. Wittenberg, *Explorations in Autism* (pp. 56–98). Strathtay: Clunie Press.

Young, E. B. (1996). A psychoanalytic approach to addiction: The formation and use of a precocious paranoid-schizoid-depressive organization. *Journal of Melanie Klein and Object Relations, 14*: 177–195

For Product Safety Concerns and Information please contact our EU representative GPSR@taylorandfrancis.com
Taylor & Francis Verlag GmbH, Kaufingerstraße 24, 80331 München, Germany

www.ingramcontent.com/pod-product-compliance
Ingram Content Group UK Ltd.
Pitfield, Milton Keynes, MK11 3LW, UK
UKHW022201190926
475702UK00003B/140
* 9 7 8 0 3 6 7 1 0 7 3 5 2 *